D1202954

BISON
BOOKS

The Road to Auschwitz

Fragments of a Life

HEDI FRIED

Edited and translated from the original Swedish by
MICHAEL MEYER

University of Nebraska Press
Lincoln and London

♾ The paper in this book meets the minimum requirements of American
National Standard for Information Sciences—Permanence of Paper for
Printed Library Materials, ANSI Z39.48-1984.

First Bison Books printing: 1996
Most recent printing indicated by the last digit below:
10   9   8   7   6   5   4   3   2   1

Library of Congress Cataloging-in-Publication Data
Fried, Hedi.
[Skärvor av ett liv. English]
The road to Auschwitz: fragments of a life / Hedi Fried; edited and trans-
lated from the original Swedish by Michael Meyer.
p.   cm.
Previously published: Fragments of a life. London: Robert Hale, 1990.
ISBN 0-8032-6893-9 (alk. paper)
1. Jews—Persecutions—Romania—Sighetu Marmatiei.   2. Holocaust,
Jewish (1939–1945)—Romania—Sighetu Marmatiei—Personal narratives.
3. Fried, Hedi.   4. Sighetu Marmatiei (Romania)—Ethnic relations.
I. Meyer, Michael Leverson.   II. Title.
DS135.R72S5313   1997
949.8'4004924—dc20
96-8536   CIP

Originally published in 1990 by Robert Hale, London.

Contents

To the memory of my mother and father,
Frida Szmuk-Klein and Ignatz Szmuk

1 Sighet

The sun is setting behind the green hills. The procession of tired men, women and children follows the slow-flowing river. There is no sound but that of shuffling feet and the scraping of sticks against stones. How many are they? People dressed in rags, with bundles on their shoulders and staffs in their hands. Women carry their infants, older children their small brothers and sisters, the men help the old. No one speaks. All that needs to be said has been said.

Where are they going? Will they find a home? Will they be allowed to stay? They believe so. I see this vision repeated again and again, Jews with bundles and staffs. I am one of them, yet stand outside and watch it all.

I no longer know if it was my mother who dreamed this dream or I. Or some ancestral figure in the mists of time. Why do I see it now, when I want to tell of my childhood in the town forgotten by God in a remote corner of the Carpathians?

I lived in Sighet. The little Transylvanian town lay at the foot of a mountain, surrounded by watercourses. The River Iza emptied its muddy waters into the spring-clear Tisza, which flowed in two arms around the town on its island. The air was thin and transparent and made everything feel near. The deep green of the forests on the mountainside was broken by fields where cattle grazed. The farmers in their peasant dress guarding the sheep seemed an arm's length away. A little town surrounded by orchards, whose trees were heavy in autumn with ripe apples and walnuts. The heart of the town was the park, with fine flower-beds in summer and a soft white coverlet of snow in winter. Around the park moved the sleepy, small-town life. People walking to church, to the cinema, to the chemist, to the bank, to school, to the butcher, to the café.

Everything centred around the park, and no one was in a hurry. On its gravelled paths walked the Catholic procession on Palm Sunday, the Virgin Mary enthroned beneath the red canopy, the small boys in white surplices swinging censers before the priest in his lilac robe, the people walking behind, singing and waving palm branches. On Twelfth Night the Greek Orthodox congregation, dressed in black, celebrated before a gigantic cross of ice. And there walked the Jews in their kaftans reaching to their toes, with white stockings and fur-rimmed hats, on the Sabbath and the Jewish holidays. Then most of the shutters would be drawn in the surrounding shops. Of the 30,000 inhabitants of the town almost half were Jews, and many of them merchants.

In the afternoons the military band played in the little pavilion. Around on the white benches elderly couples sat and listened. Maids pushed prams, keeping an eye on their older charges while they acquainted themselves with soldiers. Small boys in sailor suits chased hoops, and small girls in white socks and varnished shoes rocked their dolls to sleep.

Late in the afternoon a beggar always left the park just as the band was playing its final march. That was the signal to the shop-owners in the High Street that it was approaching seven and they could close for the day. Some had already begun to draw the heavy shutters in front of their windows and were now waiting for the church clock to strike.

My mother and I would be sitting in Uncle Samuel's textile shop, waiting for father to fetch us as soon as he had finished work. It was a tradition that we should round off the afternoon with a visit to my father's eldest brother. I always felt excited to be allowed to walk among all those gaudily coloured cloths, shining and flowered, soft and silky. I knew I would be given some samples, which mother would make into dolls' clothes.

The church clock began to strike. The sound of shutters, of cabs on the cobbles, of people on their way home, accompanied us as we began to walk back. We left the two-storeyed houses of the High Street and turned east towards Professor Street. Now it was quieter, only the chimes of the clock accompanying our footsteps. We passed the school and the pleasant villas with their small gardens in front, and came to the crossroads where the town ended. The stone-paved road curved right, then back towards the town. In front of us lay big gardens and empty fields, and to the left the hospital complex with a stone pavement before the fence. That street, named after the hospital, led to the highway which ran on through numerous local villages.

We lived at 33 Hospital Street, opposite the asylum park. On our side of the street there were no pavements. We followed the narrow trodden path between the grey fence and the muddy road to the red gate, the entrance to my childhood home, my memories.

Memories. A memory which is rather the memory of what someone told me. The incident itself has paled. I see myself standing in my parents' room, howling and angry. The year is 1926, and I am barely two years old. It is morning, the beds are not made. Father wants me to brush my teeth. I do not want to. He stands with the toothbrush in his hand. I refuse. Two wills that clash. I don't yet know it, but the outcome is determined. He is the stronger. He smacks my bottom, I cry, but still I will not. Father works himself up. He gets angrier and angrier, I more and more obstinate. He smacks and smacks until mother comes and rescues me. Did I brush my teeth then or not? I don't remember. But I remember that I had to ask to be forgiven and promise that I would never be stubborn again.

My earliest memory. I was three and was starting at kindergarten. I was happy at this, for as yet I had no brothers or sisters to play with. Mother took me there and collected me, at which I protested. Most of the children were older than I and went to school alone, and it was important that I should seem to be as clever as they. I begged and cried and in due course triumphed. Mother accompanied me to school, but I would be allowed to go home alone.

When the clock struck twelve and the teacher released us, I walked away happily with a group of children, without reflecting in which direction my home lay. Talking eagerly, I hardly noticed that they were leaving me one by one as we reached their homes. Suddenly I was standing there alone. I looked around. A muddy street like ours, the same grey fence, but no red gate. The houses were unfamiliar, and I realized that I was lost. I began to cry.

A woman stopped and asked, 'Why are you crying, little girl?'

'I can't find my home.'

'Where do you live?'

'Inside a red gate.'

'What is your name?'

'Hedike.'

'Whose child are you?'

'Daddy's.'

'Don't cry, Hedike. I will take you home.'

I stopped crying and took her hand as she turned in the direction opposite to that in which we had been going. After some minutes I began to recognize the area, and soon we were in Hospital Street, where I saw my mother standing uneasily at the window. It transpired that the woman had noticed a resemblance between me and my father, and the town was small enough for her to know where we lived.

An idyll? It seemed so on the surface. And as yet I had not scratched the surface.

They said I was a solemn child. That sounded flattering, so I was determined to live up to it. I thought it meant that one never laughed. So I did not dare to laugh. Later, when my little sister was born (in 1929) and everything centred on her, I fantasized about making an impression by my solemnity. My sister was the happy, pretty child and I the sad, ugly girl.

We had a sheltered childhood. Our parents were very loving. Child psychology was at that time an unknown science, and no one understood my jealousy. I turned in on myself and lived in my fantasies. Every word of praise for my little sister seemed a condemnation of me.

Life in Sighet went its slow way, today like yesterday, yesterday like tomorrow. In the morning we went to school, mother went to the market to shop, and father went to the factory of which he was part-owner, where they made cardboard boxes. The business prospered at first. We were comfortably off, father could give us what we needed. We could not afford any big luxury, but books and paintings, albeit inexpensive ones, were a necessity.

Not much happened in my little world. School was the most important factor. And, gradually, as the 1930s passed, the boys whom one met on the way to school. Sometimes, when the wireless was on, I would hear a strange ranting followed by alarming roars. These made my parents pensive, and I sensed their disquiet. To my questions they soothingly replied: 'It is only a madman in Germany' or 'Dogs that bark don't bite.' This did not sound wholly convincing, but anyway we lived in Romania, and Germany was so far away.

What was near was my little world, the yellow house on Hospital Street. A grey fence protected us from inquisitive eyes and unwelcome visitors. The red gate was always locked. Visitors had to pull the bellrope to gain admittance. Our mongrel, Bodri, chained to his kennel, snarled savagely as soon as anyone approached. Inside the gate was a stone-paved yard, which led to the house, the outside kitchen and the garden. There was also an earth-cellar in which food was stored, for there were no refrigerators in Sighet.

The garden was my favourite spot in summer and in winter. Along the fence were ten plum trees, whose fruit we picked in autumn. In the middle of the garden was a swing. My sister Livi and I used to fight about who should use it. Vegetable beds lay to the right, flowers on the left. Tall rose bushes, my mother's pride, flaunted their white, red, pink and yellow petals. As the seasons changed, so too did the smells – of roses, honeysuckle, jasmine, asters. Mother loved flowers and tended them lovingly.

Our home consisted of four rooms, one of which was occupied by my grandparents. Mother had been their youngest child, and grandfather bought the house for us so that they could have somewhere to spend the autumn of their years. Grandfather would sit leafing through his yellowing folio-sized books and chewing at his long-stemmed pipe. It was fun to crawl up onto his knees and play with his long white beard. He had funny nicknames for us children and could tell strange stories about the oddest things. Grandmother was gruffer. She ran the house, went to market despite her age and returned heavy-laden.

We did not have them with us for long. Grandfather died when I was five. His death shook me, the first cloud in my heaven. It was difficult to understand that he was dead, that he would never tell any more stories or dandle us on his knee. I was very sad and hid so that no one should see me crying. I was the big sister, and big, brave girls never cry.

'Mother, why is grandfather dead?'

'He was old. His heart hadn't the strength to beat any longer. It stopped.'

'Will my heart stop too?'

'Don't think about it. You're only a child.'

But I continued to worry. I went on thinking about grandfather, about death, the heart that can stop beating. At night I lay in bed and listened to my heart. Was it beating? I lay awake in fear lest it should stop while I slept.

Hardly had I got over grandfather's death when my grandmother died too. But life went on. Their room became a kitchen, so that we no longer needed to use the kitchen in a separate building in the yard. Our maid slept there, and we soon got used to the new way of things. My fear of death returned and I was allowed to sleep on the sofa in my parents' room. Normally Livi and I slept in the nursery.

We children seldom entered the fourth room. That was the dining-room, forbidden territory for us. We were only allowed into it to meet visitors. I dreamed of going into the dining-room when no one was there, of lying on the soft carpets and playing with the delicate china ballerina. I dreamed of having a ballerina of my own, but that would have to wait until I got big. I did not realize that one could save up for something. I had no pocket money. If I wanted to buy ice-cream or sweets, I had to ask for money.

At the same time it was impressed on me that I must never accept money from strangers. The town was full of tramps, and we feared these ugly old men. So I was unsure what to do when offered a coin by the judge, whom I had never met before. I was playing with a neighbour's daughter of my age called Baba when another neighbour, Aunt Kostencki (it was a Romanian custom to call elders 'Aunt' or 'Uncle') told us to run over to the town hall with a letter to the judge, her husband. We did and as reward were each handed a shining 20 lei coin. Baba accepted hers with a happy smile, but I braced myself and refused. Father's warning whispered in my ears: 'Never accept money from old men you haven't met.' The judge urged me, Baba cajoled, I shook my head but in the end I gave in and took it.

When I was out in the street, I looked at my new-found wealth and wondered what I should do with it. I did not dare to tell anyone at home, for fear I would be punished.

I went to the grocer's and asked if I could buy chocolate to the full amount of so large a sum. The grocer smiled and nodded, but I did not dare believe him. I thought he was trying to trick me. I could not imagine a bar of chocolate so big that it could cost 20 lei. I thought it safest to buy some other sweets, and asked for acid drops. The grocer looked at me in some surprise and weighed out a large bag. I had never seen so many sweets, and my mouth watered. Quickly I popped one into my mouth and began to suck. It tasted marvellous. The smooth, slightly sharp, fruity taste caressed my palate and ran down into my stomach. I took the sweet out for a moment, to remind myself what colour it was. It was red. I sucked on till it was finished, then went on to a green one. It tasted of woods and summer. The next was yellow and tasted of orange. The fourth seemed less good, and I had difficulty with the fifth.

Now I realized that I would not be able to eat any more

and would have to hide the rest. But where? It would need to be at home, in a safe place so that no one would find them. I went back, hoping no one would see me before I had hidden the bag away. 'Please God, let the gate be open,' I prayed all the way home. God was kind to me. The gate was open and I could tiptoe into the dining-room, where I hid the bag at the bottom of the china-cupboard. And forgot all about it.

A few weeks later Uncle Fischman, Baba's father, came to visit us. When he saw me, he asked: 'Well, what have you done with your money?'

Then I remembered the sweets I had hidden in the china-cupboard. I flushed and wanted to run off. Mother grabbed hold of me and asked, 'What money?'

'The 20 lei she got from Judge Kostencki when Baba and she took him the letter,' replied Uncle Fischman.

Mother looked at me doubtingly: 'Have you had money from Judge Kostencki?'

'Didn't you tell your mother?' asked Uncle Fischman.

'Well, what is it you haven't told us?' said mother impatiently, giving me a stern look.

I was frightened but understood that there was no way out. I had to tell. I confessed that I had accepted 20 lei, and to my great surprise no storm erupted. Mother was not angry. She only wanted to know where I had put the money. When I told her the whole story, she became upset because I had wasted my money on sweets. She wanted to see the bag. We went into the dining-room in Indian file, I first, then mother, with Uncle Fischman bringing up the rear. When I opened the door of the china-cupboard, I could not believe my eyes. There was a sticky bag covered with millions of crawling ants. Mother looked at it and must have decided that it was sufficient punishment for me that the sweets would have to be thrown away.

Our home was sparingly furnished, and we had no bathroom. Several years passed before father could afford to buy a modern house with a bathroom and parquet floors. Until then we had to bathe in a wooden tub, which was placed on two rib-backed chairs in the kitchen every Thursday evening. The water was heated on the stove, and the steam stood thick about us. The smell of the brown beans for dinner remained, mixed with that of dough fermenting by the stove in soft plaited baskets. All the bread we needed for the week was baked on Friday morning. Livi and I quarrelled about who would sit at the end of the tub where the plug was. In the end we agreed that whichever of us had the most cuts on our legs should have the most comfortable place. We counted our wounds and, once agreed, we were washed, dried and tucked away in our soap-scented sheets.

As I lay waiting for sleep, fears crept forth. Usually they took the form of peasants from the villages, peasants in their Sunday best with several hats on their heads. Why was I so frightened of them? I was used to seeing peasants in their colourful folk-dress, for they came daily to town to sell their goods in the market. On Fridays, when they had finished trading, they went to the shops to make their own purchases of clothes and other necessities. They put these new clothes on – it was easier than carrying them. Then they went to the inn, and when I met them with their many hats on they were usually drunk. Was it the drunken things they would talk of when they thought the children were out of earshot? Their tattle of Jews whose beards they had pulled, of children who could not go in peace to Cheder – to learn the Hebrew alphabet, of peasants who threw stones at prayer-houses and overturned gravestones in the Jewish burial ground?

Winter was usually harsh. I can still feel the cold that bit my cheeks as I walked home from my piano lessons in the evening dark. The stars sparkled, the moon cast long shadows and, as the snow crunched beneath my boots, I warmed my hands on the hot chestnuts I had in my pockets. At the street corner there stood an old man who roasted chestnuts in a rusty red urn, and I could never walk by him, however much I was in a hurry. The glowing eyes of the coals hypnotized me and made me stop, oblivious of the cold. If I had a coin, I bought a package; otherwise I simply stood and inhaled the smell.

In the square in front of the theatre was a skating-rink, and I was happy when father gave me a pair of skates so that I could join in. Uncle Laci ran the rink and kept a fire burning in a little shed where we could put on our skates and rest between-times. He was always willing to help us screw our skates tight, and he cranked the rickety gramophone to whose notes the ice-princesses swayed. 'The Skaters' Waltz', 'The Blue Danube' and other languid melodies lent wings to the girls who danced in short, fur-lined velvet skirts. It took time for me to learn, and I envied the girls who pirouetted and traced figures as darkness fell and the lamps were lit. Mostly, I played tag with the boys and often ran in to Uncle Laci to warm myself and listen to his stories. He sold tea and hot toddy and liked to tell of his exploits in the First World War.

But the winter was short. Soon the candles of the horse-chestnuts flamed outside our windows. The days grew longer, and it was still light when I returned from my piano lessons. Cockchafers swarmed among the treetops, their amber wings glittering in the setting sun. They soughed and droned, and small children spiked the wretched creatures on sticks to play at aeroplanes. I bargained for the lives of the dying insects, sacrificing my most precious treasures, my prettiest stones, but to small purpose, for soon the children captured new victims, stuffed them in a matchbox and ran off to continue their games elsewhere.

The cherry trees blossomed and the bees sang in the asylum park. Figures in grey hospital uniform strolled past, their dreaming faces lifted towards the trees. I remember especially a man with sparse grey hair whom I often saw, his body stooped, walking with heavy steps, a harrowed expression and a wandering stare. He kept turning round as though he thought someone was following him. He walked slowly, gesturing and chatting to himself. Suddenly his eyes seemed to be caught by something, and his wandering stare would fix itself on a tree-top. His expression froze and he might stand there with wide-open eyes, half-open mouth and hunched shoulders, motionless for hours. What was he seeing? Did the tree's beauty bewitch him, or did he glimpse something terrible behind the foliage? A future from which he was fleeing but which yet might sink its claws into him?

The flowers withered, the weather grew warmer and red cherries appeared. One Saturday I was wakened by the sun tickling my face and saw through the window the hospital janitor picking the ripe fruit. Will he give me some, I wondered, and jumped out of bed. I put on my best clothes, my new white woollen dress embroidered with cats, and my black patent leather shoes. I begged to be allowed to wear short socks, but mother did not think it was warm enough. She decided that I must also wear my new coat, of red, white and grey check, and I felt very smart in it. I knotted a red scarf around my neck to go with the blue rosette in my hair. Outside on the street, happy with my appearance, I hoped to attract the janitor's attention. I stood in front of the fence with pleading eyes, my hands on the barbed wire.

After a moment the janitor turned to me and said: 'Would you like some cherries?'

'Yes, please ...'

'Get a basket and you shall have some.'

I ran in to mother, shouting happily: 'A basket, a basket! I'm getting some cherries!'

I ran back with the basket, and Uncle Jancsi, the hospital janitor, held a stick over the fence to lift it over. He filled the basket with cherries and gave it back to me by the same method. I thanked him and began to look for 'earrings', cherries that were joined together. When I had found two, I hung them over my ears and ran back home to give two others to my little sister. I handed the basket to mother without tasting a single cherry.

I waited impatiently for father to return from synagogue so that we could have lunch and then at last be able to eat them. I ran to the street corner and back time and again, hoping he would come more quickly if I went to meet him. At last I saw him turning in to our street, big and blond, with smiling blue eyes. He stretched out his arms when he saw me running and lifted me up. My stomach tickled as he whirled me round and threw me up into the air.

'More! more!' I cried in a mixture of fear and delight.

After a moment he put me back on the ground, and we walked home, my little hand in his big fist. I looked up at him and proudly thought that no one had such a wonderful father as I. He was handsome, he was wise, he was strong, he was gentle. I loved my father more than anything in the world.

When I was older, I often thought how unjust I had been in my love. It was mother who looked after us children, who stayed at home all day, kept the house and saw that everything was in order. When father came home, it was just fun and games, happiness and laughter. He did not have to be strict, for the problems that had arisen during the day were already solved. None the less, I worshipped my father, while somehow imagining that my mother was my stepmother.

Now my father was home I laughed with joy, chattered away, told as quickly as I could all that had happened to me. Soon my little sister would come and claim her share of my father's love.

When we entered the dining-room, the Sabbath meal was already laid. The traditional cholet* had already been fetched from the baker's and stood majestically on the white damask tablecloth. Father blessed us before reading the prayer over the bread. We seated ourselves around the table and began on the chopped liver, while mother questioned father about how his day had gone and whom he had met. I picked at my food, willing them to hurry; I could think only of the cherries. After an eternity they at last arrived on the table and I ate them happily. Mother and father were tired after the heavy meal and went into the bedroom to lie down.

'Can you be quiet while we sleep?' asked mother.

'Yes,' we answered.

'If you are really good, we can go for a walk afterwards,' said my father.

'Just you and me?' I asked.

'Whose turn is it?'

'Mine,' said Livi and I simultaneously.

On Saturdays father used to take one of us for a little walk. It was the best thing I knew, to have father alone with me. That was when he told all the exciting stories about his childhood, of strange animals, and the war, and the great world which lay far away. This time Livi would not accept that it was my turn, so we began to quarrel. Father said he thought it was my turn and promised Livi that she could do something else exciting instead. She

---

* A dish of beans and barley which we left on Friday at the baker's. Fire must not be lit on the Sabbath, so this was the only way to have hot food.

could go with mother to the park and show off her new doll's pram.

Mother and father went to lie down and we were as quiet as mice. We did not want to risk losing the thrills ahead. We went out into the garden to play until our parents woke, and then we dressed for the walk.

'Father, will you die?'

'Everyone must die.'

'I don't want you to die.'

'No one asks us. One dies when the time comes.'

'When will the time come?'

'One doesn't know beforehand. Usually it's when one has grown old. Look how lovely everything is now. The grass is growing, everything is in flower. In the autumn, when everything has grown old, it withers and dies. But soon the spring comes again, and then the new grass grows, and new flowers, and the trees get new leaves. It is the same with us mortals. The old ones die, new ones are born. There would be no room for the new children if the old people did not die.'

'But I don't want grandfather to be dead.'

'I think grandfather was content to die. He was old and tired, and I think he felt it would be good to fall asleep and not have to wake up.'

'Sometimes he comes to the window and looks in.'

'No, when one is dead, one cannot come back.'

'But if we think about him, he exists.'

'Yes, I suppose that's true.'

'Look, father, a beetle.'

'Yes, look how beautiful it is.'

'What big horns it has.'

'It is a stag beetle,' father explained, and he began to tell me about different beetles. Death was forgotten. So much that was exciting happened on our walks.

In the summer I was taken to the country to stay with
my aunt and uncle. They had a little farm and toiled from
morning till evening. With primitive tools and no help
worth mentioning, how did they manage?

Yet somehow they found room and time for all their
nephews and nieces.

Both mother and father came from big families. Apart
from children who had died in infancy, they each had six
brothers and sisters living, and each of those had between
two and five children. The family was tightly knit, and we
all met often. Father's brothers and sisters lived in Sighet,
but mother's were scattered throughout various towns in
Transylvania. Only Aunt Regina lived in the country, and
it was regarded as a good thing for town children to be
sent into the countryside for a spell. Aunt Regina became
our summer mother and accepted us with great patience
and love. Lăpuşel, where she lived, was a small farming
village containing about thirty families. Many of these
were Jews living in peaceful harmony with their
Romanian neighbours. Until compulsory education was
introduced, there was a Jewish school in Lapusel, and
several of the more enlightened local Gentiles sent their
children there.

Before discrimination began, Aunt Regina's husband
owned a little country store and wine tavern. I still
remember how he measured out the shining sweets into
twists of brown wrapping-paper, beneath hanging
paraffin lamps amid the odour of spices. In the next room,
the wine tavern with its wooden floor and blue walls, sat
the villagers on wooden benches with bottles of schnapps
before them. The vapour of the spirits mingled with the
smell of sweat and of the cowhouse, and the level of noise
rose higher and higher. The hum of conversation turned
into loud debate, and someone began to sing. Melancholy
love-songs alternated with rhythmic military marches,

and when someone took up his fiddle they jumped up to join in a merry dance. There were no women there, and children were not permitted. When I had got my twist of sweets and wanted to go into the wine tavern, I was immediately stopped. Jews never went to the wine tavern, least of all Jewish children.

All year I longed for the country, and I was happy when at last I saw the blue houses with their straw roofs, the barn with its carved doors, and the muddy yard with its characteristic well. Not much happened in the country. Now that I look back, it was one long summer day, sunny and hot, with occasional showers of rain that smelled of old wood and sunflower seeds. I played with baby goats, drank warm milk from the cow and bathed in the muddy river among the black water-buffaloes. Great was my joy when I saw the friends I had made there last year, and we could talk of everything that had happened since we had parted. We acted plays in the barn, played on swings, borrowed each other's books and went on journeys of exploration along the river. I did not feel homesick, yet it was exciting to go to the post office every day to see if a letter had come.

When it rained, I could hide myself in the loft with all the old books. The best fun was to leaf through old magazines with pictures from the previous century, but I read everything that came into my hands, whether I understood it or not: Balzac, *The Odyssey*, children's stories, all in a glorious confusion. The rain pattered soothingly on the roof, but when the thunder began to growl, I became frightened. I dared not wait for the lightning but ran down to the kitchen, where my aunt was shutting all the windows. We sat on the bed in the darkest corner of the room, and in scared anticipation I asked her to tell me yet again the story of the fireball that came in through the window.

It had happened during the First World War. Uncle was serving in the Austro-Hungarian Army, which was fighting in Bosnia. He was in a barracks in the midst of the forest and was operating the Morse telegraph when a big fireball appeared in the open window, floated slowly forward, was sucked into the telephone and vanished. My uncle was paralysed with fear. He was sure it was a manifestation of the devil. This fear remained with him all his life, and he transmitted it to his close and even to his more distant relatives.

Uncle taught me a prayer to say when the thunder growled, and another for when the lightning flashed, as protection against the fireball. I was very frightened, hid myself under the pillows and mechanically repeated these prayers again and again. It did not help that my aunt said I should pray only once, the first time I heard the thunder. I did not stop until the last rumble had died away and the sun appeared.

Such storms changed the dust in the yard to a mud porridge. When we went out, our shoes sank deep. The washed air tempted us to walk, and I did not mind that I would have a hard cleaning job to do on my shoes afterwards. We kept to the highway and tried to avoid the worst puddles. Our greatest joy was to walk to the bridge and back. We did not have to worry about traffic, for there were few vehicles to be seen.

The summer passed quickly. Soon the days became shorter, the weather cooler, and the school term approached. It was time to go home. I began to pack, to gather together the treasures I had assembled during the summer: pine-cones, polished stones, feathers and bright necklaces of dried berries. Towards evening, when the cow-bells began to tinkle, I ran to the barn to drink the foaming milk for the last time that summer. After the milking my uncle harnessed Snow White and Rosa to the cart and took us to the nearby town to catch the bus for Sighet. The oxen moved slowly, and it was late in the evening when we reached my cousin's, where I was to spend the night.

My cousin lived in a little rented room opposite the church on the upper floor of a two-storey house. The clock in the church tower kept me company and was the first thing I saw when my cousin woke me in the grey dawn. I heard the pigeons cooing as they perched on the windowsill to greet me. We had no pigeons in Sighet, and I could not understand why my cousin shooed them away. I dressed quickly and we went to the café in the square, where I had hot chocolate and fresh croissants while we waited for the bus. When it arrived, I was handed over to the driver and told not to move from my seat until we had reached Sighet.

Out on the highway the bus gathered itself for the climb up Mount Gutin. Coughing and blowing, it crawled up the narrow, winding road lined with deciduous trees which gradually gave way to pines. The bus had no springs to speak of, and I was shaken up and down like a medicine bottle. Often someone felt sick, and then the bus had to stop and wait while he or she got off to vomit. The landscape spread beneath us in ever-increasing vistas the higher we climbed. The houses grew smaller and smaller as we approached the pass and were soon invisible. The winding roads beneath us looked like snakes crawling in the greenness. Once we had reached the pass, the bus stopped and we could get out to stretch our legs and drink the murmuring spring water. By the spring was a crucified Christ on a carved wooden cross. Many of the passengers knelt to offer thanks that the bus had brought us safely to the top, and to pray for a safe descent. The clouds half-enveloped the ghostlike figures by the roadside, and it was as though all sound was muffled in cotton-wool.

Not many people spoke. The altitude and the damp air made us want to get down, and soon everyone was back in their seats.

The bus re-started, and its blowing and stuttering changed to a contented hum as it began to descend the pass. The deeper we descended into the valley, the more animated the passengers became. Cautious words began to be exchanged, and soon there was a buzz of conversation. People who had previously been silent chatted and offered each other apples and sandwiches. The clouds lifted and the sun appeared. The pines vanished and glades of deciduous trees greeted the homebound bus. We drove past the little watch-house in the valley and met the farmers in their peasant dress leading their cattle to grazing.

When the first carved wooden gates appeared, so typical of the Maramureş region, I knew we would soon be in Sighet. I recognized the familiar sights, the villages, the clock-tower, the waterfall whose gurgling accompanied us, Uncle Michael's orchard with its walnut and apple trees. I looked forward to going there as soon as possible to pick the ripe fruit and taste the soft peeled walnut kernels. It was best to pick them before the green rind had come away; it didn't matter that the shell made one's hands black. I wanted the driver to stop but knew that was impossible. I had to be patient; we would soon be there.

Now we had reached the outskirts of the town. The shops were open. It was market day, and farmers from the villages thronged the streets with sacks on their backs. They would sell vegetables, eggs, chickens, cheese and milk and buy fine cloths and other luxuries which the town had to offer. Women in striped aprons and vivid scarves stood out among the white-clad men. A farmer sat on a horse-drawn cart and swished his whip. The bus drove by them, enveloping everything in a cloud of dust. We passed my Uncle Pinchas's restaurant, Uncle Samuel's textile shop, and now I saw mother and Livi waving at the approaching bus. It stopped in the square, the door opened, and we fell into each other's arms. I was eager to tell of everything I had done, and Livi wanted to tell me about her summer. Mother had difficulty getting a word in and had to be content to listen while we seated ourselves in a cab and drove home to Hospital Street.

I remember especially one homecoming, an autumn when I was greeted with two big pieces of news. Uncle Michael had been nominated as a Liberal candidate for Parliament, and we were moving to a new house.

It was 1938. The country was governed by the Farmers' Party, which was anti-Semitic, so that the life of Jews in the towns and villages was far from calm. Injustices, harassment, stone-throwing and fights became everyday occurrences. The Liberals, who sought the Jewish vote, promised to fight anti-Semitism and as a token of their goodwill included this Jew, my Uncle Michael, in their nominations list. The election was to be held in a couple of months, and all Jews were hoping for a Liberal victory. I felt proud of my uncle.

But the other piece of news overshadowed his nomination. We were moving. Father had at last bought the house we had so long coveted: the house on Station Street which looked like a matchbox with a flat roof and which we had never dared to believe we could ever afford to buy.

In the days which followed, we could talk of nothing but the house and our impending move. The house comprised five rooms and a loft, which Livi and I immediately claimed as ours. It was independent of the rest of the house, being reached by a spiral staircase direct from the front door. I noted with pleasure that we would not have to go through our parents' room to reach it. The room facing the yard was to be their bedroom, the one in the middle the dining-room, and that facing the street the parlour. New furniture was to be bought, and in our imagination we furnished the house again and again. At last we would have room for a piano. 'Father, you promise to buy a piano? Do you really promise?' We were to have a fine sofa, and a cupboard for books and glasses which the carpenter had promised to copy exactly from an illustration I had seen in a furniture magazine. It would all be very grand.

Livi and I went to the house at least once a day, scampering among, and inconveniencing, the workmen who were finishing the improvements. In a week it would be ready for us to move in. I especially admired the bathroom, with its shining white tub flush with the floor, the china hand-basin with taps marked 'Hot' and 'Cold', and the big brown water-heater in the corner, standing guard over everything. Imagine, waking in the morning and being able to take a hot bath! Just turn the tap. It wasn't really that simple. First you had to stand in the kitchen and pump water for half an hour, then lay and light a fire under the heater, and finally the bath would be ready. But what a luxury then, to stretch one's limbs in wonderful hot water.

Porcelain stoves stood in the various rooms. The one in the dining-room had white tiles, with a recess for a flower vase; the one in the parlour was lime green, and the one in the bedroom pale rose. There was no tiled stove in the loft, only a little iron one, which made the room somehow more inviting. We chose light colours and small patterns for the walls. I was tired of the dark colours and large patterns of the walls in Hospital Street. The mauve bunches of lilac had been fine when I was small, but now I was a teenager, and my taste had changed. I wanted light colours and firm lines. Functionalism had come to Sighet. How? Whence? I don't know. Magazines must have influenced me, but I fancied I had discovered it by myself.

Mother planned the garden with the help of a master gardener. Behind the house she would have her kitchen garden and some fruit trees. In front, facing the street, were to be a lawn, flower-beds and Japanese cherries. The fence was of open squares, so that we could have contact with the street, not hide ourselves, as previously, behind a high wall – perhaps because it was more centrally situated, with less danger of burglars, perhaps because we wanted to show off our pretty house with its fine garden. Station Street was for the well-to-do, the houses were large and expensive, and the owners competed to show who had the finest flowers. They did not have to do the gardening themselves; labour was very cheap.

Anna's parents had the finest garden on our street. Anna was a cousin who became my best friend once we had moved there. She was dark, with raven-black plaits coiled down her back, aristocratic-looking with lovely curved lips. Her nose was straight and gave her a slightly spiteful expression. Large, innocent blue eyes looked at you from behind dark eyelashes and became alluring when she smiled. As she grew older, all the boys' eyes turned to her, and I hoped that some of her glamour might rub off on me. I always chose my friends from the prettiest girls.

In 1938 I was fourteen, Anna sixteen. She was keen that we should take the air in the High Street, but I did not see what fun that would be. The school rules were very strict, and all the usual small-town pleasures, such as going to the cinema and walking with boys, were forbidden to us pupils. So we had to exploit the only pleasure left. Girls walked with girls and ogled the boys. This was something new to me, but I was unwilling to admit my inexperience and promised Anna I would walk with her once I had finished my lessons. I looked at my books and decided I had not too much to do that afternoon. The history was easy, I knew French, only the arithmetic would take time. But soon I had done that too, and when Anna telephoned I grabbed my school cap and ran to the door.

Once the shops had shut, the High Street between the church and the cinema was transformed into a promenade. The girls in their school uniforms walked arm in arm, leaving from in front of the church as the boys reached the cinema, so that they could meet halfway. The girls wore black dresses with white collars, black stockings, black shoes and dark blue berets, the boys army-green suits and green peaked caps with the school badge. We glanced surreptitiously at one another, the braver among us whispering a word or two as the two groups passed. It was usually a boy who did this; the girls pretended not to notice them. But all was carefully registered, every glance, every gesture; nothing escaped us. Afterwards for hours we would recall and discuss every glance, every gesture, every word.

Our walks became more relaxed, and one day as I walked past a schoolboy something stirred in my breast. He had a beautiful, softly smiling face, and when I looked at him I felt something unusual. A curious, pleasant, soothing yet upsetting feeling. Who could he be? I had fallen in love with someone whose name I did not even know.

Now the walks became important for me too. I walked up and down the High Street to see him, in the hope that he might notice me. I discovered his address, his school, his habits, and all my energy went into working out where and when I could meet him. It didn't matter that we didn't know each other. I walked on a cloud as soon as I caught sight of him, and almost fainted the first time he looked at me. At home I sat for hours, my books unopened, weaving dreams of love and eternal happiness.

Dreams. Ever since I was little, I had told myself stories. Each evening, before I fell asleep, I imagined stories about living dolls that I could take care of. Later, as I grew bigger, I dreamed of travelling to different lands, of discoveries and achievements.

I would become a doctor and travel round the world. I wanted to see distant lands, climb mountains, swim in seas, visit natives in Africa and help people everywhere. But travel is dangerous – suppose I should risk death? Would I dare to expose myself to that? Yes, I loved the idea of adventure and wanted to make a pact with God: 'I accept whatever trials You like, as long as I am allowed to live.' Evening after evening I thought about these future hardships and began to prepare myself. I would toughen myself to cope with climatic conditions. In winter I slept with my window open and only a single, thin blanket over me, in summer with my window shut and a thick eiderdown. I tried to inure myself to doing without food and avoided eating, so that after a time mother began to worry.

Was there something in me that sensed what lay ahead? The political situation was chaotic, the idea of war so scared me that I did not dare even to think of it. An instinct for self-preservation shielded me from reality.

Anna was always bright in the mornings and would come to see me before I got up. On Sundays I liked to lie late with a book. If mother had let me, I would have lain there reading all day.

One morning, when Anna was to collect me to go with her to the dentist, I was so absorbed by a Dumas novel, *The Count of Monte Cristo*, that I refused to accompany her. We agreed instead to meet in town at eleven o'clock. She left, and I continued to suffer with the Count on his island. I took pen and paper and practised writing with my left hand in case I should ever find myself in his predicament. Time passed, and when it was almost eleven, I jumped out of bed and dressed in haste. As I reached the gate, I saw Anna coming towards me. I was surprised she was not waiting for me in town and went to greet her with an excuse on my lips. But before I could say anything, she cried: 'War has been declared!'

'It's not true.'

'I've just been to the dentist. They have a wireless and have heard the news.'

'I don't believe it. You're making it up.'

'No, honest.'

'Oh God, how frightful!'

'What will happen to us?'

'Our fathers will be called up.'

'There'll be shooting here in the streets.'

'We may all die.'

'No, everyone doesn't die in a war. We'll be all right.'

'I'm frightened.'

'So am I.'

'We'll carve today's date on the gate and promise that whatever happens we'll meet here when the war's over, to carve that date too.'

'Yes, let's do that.'

I ran into the house, found a pocket knife and carved on the wood: 1 September 1939.

When the war ended, neither Anna nor I was in Sighet. Nor was there any gate left to carve on. Later I heard it had been burned during the war. There had been a shortage of wood.

In the autumn of 1940, when I was still only sixteen, the great world began to come close to us. Prior to 1918, Transylvania had been part of the Austro-Hungarian

Empire. The Treaty of Versailles that year had given it to Romania; now it was to be returned to Hungary. There was great rejoicing among the Hungarian minority in Romania, and among the older Jews, who regarded themselves as Hungarian. Our parents had never accepted the Romanians. Hungarian was spoken in every Jewish home, and Jews embraced Hungarian culture as a matter of course.

The school had had a problem. There were very few Romanian pupils, but none of us was allowed to talk Hungarian. We were fined for every Hungarian word we uttered. All this had taken time, but at length our teachers had succeeded in turning us Jewish children into Romanian patriots who looked down on our 'Hungarian' parents. Thus, while our parents rejoiced, we children were sad and hoped that Hungarian rule would be only temporary.

Things began to happen in Sighet. The leading Romanians in the town wanted to leave, and hitherto despised Hungarians sensed that their renaissance had begun. The shops began to run out of red, white and green fabrics, as everyone sewed flags and prepared for the great day. A holiday was declared, all shops were to shut, everyone was to have the day off. School had not yet begun, although it was already September. I was to start in the sixth form with new, Hungarian teachers. I would miss my old teachers and my Romanian classmates, who were leaving town.

I was woken by someone climbing the stairs, opened my eyes and saw that Livi was still asleep. The September sun, making a brave attempt to warm the cool morning air, peeped in through the open window. I got up, put on my dressing-gown and opened the door. Zsuzsa, our Hungarian maid, had just closed the loft door and was on her way downstairs.

'Good morning, Zsuzsa. What are you doing up here so early?'

'I was just hanging the flag out of the window. The street is full of flags; they're fluttering so prettily. Hurry up and dress. We must go out and meet them at ten o'clock. I've made some small flags for you too – we must wave them at the soldiers.'

'I don't think I shall.'

Zsuzsa was hurt by my lack of interest. She was already dressed in her best clothes and shining with joy. Her day had dawned. Now all difficulties would disappear, and she would have a happier life. It did not occur to her that she would remain a poor servant girl whether her masters were Romanian or Hungarian.

I went into the kitchen, where my parents were seated at the breakfast table. They shared Zsuzsa's joy and tried to convince me of the advantages of a Hungarian regime. The Hungarians would protect the Jews; they knew the Jews had always fought bravely for them, and they would reward the Jews' loyalty. I drank my coffee in silence and had difficulty in understanding their enthusiasm.

Zsuzsa did not know how to make time pass. She ran back and forth, made a bed here, dusted a cupboard there and asked if she might pick flowers in the garden. She gathered a big pailful of asters and dahlias to throw to the soldiers. Again and again she urged me to go with her, but I refused.

I stayed alone at home after everyone had left. In the end, however, curiosity won, and I decided to go into the street and have a look. I dressed and went out to fetch Anna. We walked to the corner of Hospital Street to await the Hungarians, who were to march in along the highway. It was ten o'clock, and the pavements were crowded with excited people carrying flags and flowers. The Hungarian flag hung in every window and there was a feeling of happy anticipation in the air. The official reception was to take place in the city park, but the people wanted to welcome the troops as soon as they approached the town's outskirts. They cheered and sang patriotic songs as they awaited their liberators.

Before long a cloud of dust in the distance announced that the soldiers were at hand. Soon I could discern the leading column, their banner aloft. Cheering broke out as the soldiers approached, singing the Rákóci March. Adults and children, Hungarians and Jews, waved, shouted and sang, threw flowers and kisses. Girls flung their arms round the soldiers' necks, kissing and hugging them. Everyone accompanied them to the park, where the official reception committee was waiting. The town's Hungarian gentry sat on the platform which had been erected for the occasion, and Biró Antal, the self-appointed burgomaster, walked up and down with a piece of paper in his hand, sweat gathering on his forehead as he rehearsed his speech. The schoolmaster exhorted his pupils to sing their best and threatened reprisals if they did not do him justice. He was having a hard job controlling them. Everyone felt relief when the Rákóci March was at last heard. The schoolmaster struck up a Hungarian folk-tune, and as soon as the soldiers came into sight the children began to sing. The troops formed up in front of the platform, and the burgomaster began his speech of welcome. Anna and I left to take a stroll in the Mill Park.

This euphoria continued for several days, but soon the old routine established itself. School started and I began to adapt to the Hungarian curriculum, new teachers and new classmates. Meanwhile the madman on the wireless (we had bought a new one) became even shriller. Austria, Czechoslovakia and Poland had been occupied, and there were rumours of atrocities against dissidents and Jews.

Did we know of the concentration camps? I don't remember.

What I do remember is a Jewish refugee from Poland who came to our little town and was hidden by Aunt Lotti, long before the Hungarians arrived. He sat in a darkened room, starting up whenever anyone knocked on the door. We children were allowed to take food to him, and I was frightened by his wandering stare, which mirrored terror, timidity and pain. There was so much I would have liked to ask him, to tell him. I wanted to comfort him, but I could not speak his language. My parents answered my questions evasively, whispering to each other of horrors he had escaped, but I don't think anyone believed that such things might affect us. What had happened had happened in Germany, in Austria, in Czechoslovakia, in Poland, not in Hungary. We were Hungarian citizens; our fathers had fought in the Hungarian Army in the First World War. As a child I had played with father's medals for bravery. Nothing could happen to us.

I lived as before, did my lessons, wrote my diary, met friends and dreamed of love. Dreamed of Him with a capital H whom I met every day on my way to school. Dreamed and hoped that one day I might be noticed by him, that my feelings would be reciprocated. He was tall and slim, and each morning I offered a prayer that his blue eyes should meet mine. I held my breath as I walked past him, but he was always busy discussing something with another boy. Then one day, as I returned from school, it happened. For once he was alone. I saw him and slowed my pace. My heart raced, my knees went weak. Now, now he will see me, perhaps he will greet me, perhaps even walk a few yards with me. He approached whistling, his eyes met mine and as we came level he spat. Not furtively, as one does when one has a cold, not in the gutter, not casually. Deliberately, with an expression of loathing, into my face.

A world tumbled. I was scum, a dirty Jewess. What I had heard of as happening to other people in other countries had now happened to me.

I ran home crying. Mother was frightened.

'What has happened? Have you failed in arithmetic?'

'He spat at me?'

'Who?'

'That handsome boy I used to meet on the way to school.'

'You don't need to howl about that,' said mother unfeelingly.

'Mother, don't you understand?'

'I understand, but worse things can happen.'

'No, mother, nothing could be worse.'

'You know they don't like us. These things happen. You mustn't take it so hard.'

'Has it ever happened to you?'

'Not exactly, but other things have. One gets used to it.'

'I don't intend to.'

Father, who had just returned for lunch, heard my crying and came up to my room.

'What has happened?' he asked.

'Some damned anti-Semitic boy has spat at her,' said mother. 'She seems not have come across this kind of thing before.'

'Poor child. Well, she'll learn to accept that we live in an anti-Semitic world.'

'No, father, I don't want to accept it. I don't want to live in a country where people get spat at. Why don't we do something? Why are we sitting here? Why didn't we move long ago? Dear father, promise we'll go away from here.'

'That isn't so simple,' he said. 'When we could have, we didn't dare give up a safe income, a nice home, family and friends. Now there are hundreds of thousands of people who want to leave this country. It's very difficult.'

I was inconsolable. I didn't want to be like my parents, I didn't want to accept all this. I wanted to do something – run away, leave the country. In the end I had to accept that there was no possibility of this. One could only do as everyone else did – bury one's head in the sand and go on as before. But this now became harder and harder. New decrees were issued daily which made life more difficult, and in some cases impossible, for us Jews. Proclamations were drummed at street corners, and as soon as we heard the drums we knew that some new burden would be laid on our already bowed shoulders. The following orders were announced one after another:

1. Jews are forbidden to own wireless receivers. All such must be surrendered to the authorities within twenty-four hours.
2. Jews must surrender all jewels and valuables. Disobedience will be punished.
3. All vehicles owned by Jews shall immediately be handed over for use by the Army.
4. Jews are forbidden to visit restaurants, cinemas, tennis courts and bathing-places.
5. Jews are forbidden to work in public institutions.
6. Jews may not employ non-Jews. Christian girls who work in Jewish households must leave immediately.
7. Citizens may patronize only Aryan shops and are advised to have no dealings whatsoever with Jews.
8. Jewish children are not entitled to higher education.
9. All Jews must present documents to the authorities testifying that they were born in Hungary. Jews not born in Hungary will be deported to their country of origin [this usually meant Poland].

Aryanization had begun.
Proclamation 8 affected me most. The school which I

had attended for seven years was now closed to me a year before I was due to matriculate. I was deeply unhappy and begged to be allowed to move to some other town which had a Jewish school.

My parents sympathized and tried to arrange for me to move to Cluj, the capital of Transylvania. I knew that this involved financial sacrifice. The school fees, books, travel and accommodation amounted to a considerable sum. I knew it was becoming ever more difficult for Jews to earn money. But I was determined to find cheap lodgings and reward their generosity by becoming the best in my class.

A few days before term began, I went to Cluj to look for accommodation. I was sad to leave my family, though happy to be able to continue with my schooling. It was the first time I had gone away on my own, to stand on my own feet. I was to spend the first few nights with relations. They did not welcome me very warmly and although they had a large apartment were not willing to put me up for long. I was homesick but did not want anyone to know it. Although I had promised father to write on my arrival, I decided not to do so until I had found cheap lodgings.

Sighet, 2 September 1941

Dear little mischief,

You have scarcely left and are already disobedient. You know how worried we become if you are not home by eight o'clock, and can imagine how we feel now. Or have you sent a telegram which has not reached us? I enclose a paper registering your change of domicile; you will need this. I would have preferred not to send it until we had heard from you. Write and tell us about everything. Bözsi has already written to her parents. She is paying only 20 pengö for her school fees. You mustn't pay more.

Many kisses from
Your Father

My dearest child,

We are waiting so impatiently to know that you have arrived safely, but still have heard nothing. We don't know where you are living, what you are eating. We feel very worried. You were sad to leave us and we were sad to lose you, but we must get used to it if this is what you want. May God guide you.

Write often. I hope to hear from you tomorrow. Many loving hugs and kisses from

Your Mother

In the end I found lodgings with Janka, a wrinkled old woman who lived in a small room with a stove in the corner behind the door. The room also contained a bed, a sofa, a cupboard, a little table and four chairs. She already had one lodger, a university student, and I had to sleep in a camp bed, which by day was folded away beneath her bed. In the evening the table and chairs were piled away to make room for the camp bed. It was confined but cheap, and Janka cooked very good food. I was young, and these humble surroundings matched my romantic dreams of student life, based on a novel I had read about *fin-de-siècle* Paris.

So now one of my self-imposed conditions had been met, cheap lodgings. The other, to be best in my class, proved more difficult. It was not so easy to hold one's own in a class where most of the pupils seemed geniuses. Nor was I readily accepted by them. Most of them had worked together for twelve years, and they were cool to an outsider.

My first day at school began on a beautiful September morning, and I went with mixed feelings of joy and anxiety. How would it go? Would they accept me? I asked my way to the classroom and went in. The windows were open, and the girls stood chatting in groups. No one noticed me. I gathered my courage and said, 'Hullo. My name's Hedi. I'm from Sighet and will be with you for a year.'

'Hullo,' answered a few voices indifferently.

I looked around for a free desk. Finding one, I sat down at it.

'You can't sit there. That's Marianne's place.'

'But no one's sitting here.'

'She's ill today.'

'Where shall I sit?' I looked round timidly.

A girl's voice at the back said, 'You can sit with me.'

I went over and gave her my hand gratefully.

'My name's Hedi. What's yours?'

'Manyi. Are you good at German? It's my worst subject.'

'I don't know any German at all. But we can help each other.'

'Where do you live?'

'On Deák Street. Where do you?'

'On Deák Street too.'

'What luck. We can do our homework together.'

'Manyi.' An icy voice suddenly interrupted us. 'Don't forget the party at Peter's on Saturday. I promised we'd come. It's a dance.'

'Can Hedi come too?'

'No,' said the voice firmly. This, I later discovered, was Eva.

I swallowed and determined not to bother about Eva and the rest. I would just work and think of nothing else. My friendship with Manyi helped. It was good to have someone to talk to.

I worked hard. It was difficult, for the teachers were very demanding. Latin and mathematics were a special problem. But I was industrious and stubborn, and managed. I became one of the best in the class, and the other girls began to accept me. They even invited me to their parties.

After a harsh winter the term approached its end. We were all very nervous about the forthcoming matriculation. This was far from being a formality. We had written tests in Hungarian, maths and Latin, and oral examinations in the other subjects. These last took place before a five-man board chaired by the headmaster. Our chances of higher education depended on our results. That the universities were barred to Jews none of us dared consider.

A big farewell party was planned. Everyone was to go dressed as a baby. I couldn't understand the general exhilaration. I felt only a terrible emptiness. I could see no cause for rejoicing. The day of the final exam would mark the end of my childhood, and I had difficulty in imagining what would follow. I could see only a black, yawning hole, a vacuum which would swallow me; could there be anything there? However hard I tried, I could see no future. I would go home to Sighet. But then? It seemed as though life would end there.

I did not want to go to the party. I thought the other girls were being childish, and looked down on them as irresponsible. Now I understand my sense of doom, but then no one would or could understand. They called me a killjoy, and my teachers and my parents too tried to convince me that I was wrong.

In a way they were right. Life did not come to an end after the exam. I went home to Sighet and the summer vacation began as usual. But I was not willing to sit at home and enjoy a long holiday which would end only when I married. I begged my parents to let me go away again, to study to become an elementary schoolteacher. There was a Jewish seminary in Miskolc which offered a one-year course. At length they agreed. I could start at the seminary in the autumn.

But the summer remained, and now that my future was settled I let myself enjoy the holiday I had earned. I slept late in the mornings and swam daily in the river.

One day, when I got up a little earlier than usual, I happened to see my father saying his morning prayers in his bedroom. He was wearing his prayer shawl over his shoulders, and his cap, and his face was wet with tears. I could not believe my eyes. My father crying? I had never seen a man cry. I did not think men could cry. Had something happened? Had he forebodings? Did he share my sense that somehow life would end after my matriculation? But the exam was over, life had not ended. It would continue in the seminary. Why was father crying? I dared not ask. I dared not let him know that I had seen him.

Autumn arrived, and after a happy summer I went away to Miskolc. By now I had become used to separations. Nevertheless, I found it hard to leave. Although the political situation was disquieting, we felt relatively safe in little Sighet. The Germans were beginning to suffer reverses in the Soviet Union, and we thought the war might soon end. It was a grim winter, and many Jews fasted daily to get God to listen. I worked hard in the seminary and longed to go home. The letters my parents sent me often told of hardships:

Sighet, 3 March 1943

My dear child,

I should have written yesterday, but you will forgive the delay. I have been running around town all day, with a million things to do. As you know, we have to get hold of all these birth certificates for every member of the family, living or dead, including grandparents on both sides, and we can count ourselves lucky that everyone was born in Hungary. Uncle Jojlis, whose father was born in Poland, had to pay a lot to buy a false certificate. He was lucky: his papers were accepted. Rosenbaum, his neighbour, was less lucky. His forgery was discovered and he was deported with all his seven children. Who knows what will happen to him? They say the Poles do not want to have them either.

Best wishes and love from
Father

Dearest child,
    The results of your exam have arrived. I cannot tell you how happy this made us. You were afraid you would get bad marks, so we were quite unprepared. They are beyond anything we had expected. We are tremendously proud – pray God you will be able to get your just reward for this.
    Things here are so-so. Families and friends who need to arrange proof of citizenship arrive in town, and of course they have to stay with us. But with two rooms requisitioned by the military we have not much space. Our guests are rather demanding, the big house is difficult to keep clean, and although Livi helps it is too much for me. But what is all this compared to the problems which many other people have? We shall manage, provided we stay healthy.

Many hugs and kisses from
Your Mother

I returned to Sighet with my teacher's diploma. Now I no longer felt inferior. I had a profession and could always teach in a Jewish school. Once home, I learned that the first Jewish crèche had been started in town and that I could take charge of it. Most Jewish men had been conscripted and the women, left alone with their children and no means of support, were forced to look for work outside the home. To ease their problems, the crèche had been started, where children could be looked after without charge.

I was happy to have my first job, and to be earning. Even if life was circumscribed, it seemed possible to think of a future. I could begin to save for the books I wanted to buy, to plan for after the war, when the universities would again be open to us and I could begin to read medicine.

The crèche was opened in August 1943. The following March, Hungary was occupied by the Germans, and a few days later all Jews were ordered to wear the yellow star. In April we were gathered into ghettos, and in May we were transported.

2 The Ghetto

April 1944

The first journey. The journey which was not that long but which seemed all the longer. The journey on foot. The journey which was not a journey and was yet a movement between two points separated by light years. From the known to the unknown. From human warmth to the cold where the wolves lurked.

Four weeks after the German invasion in 1944, we celebrated Pesach, the Passover, which commemorates the freeing of the Jews from slavery in Egypt. We were crowded into the bedroom, for the dining-room and drawing-room were occupied by a German officer. We had already got used to being crowded, for the Hungarians had requisitioned the rooms a year previously. When the Germans came, all that happened was that the Hungarian baron moved out and a German officer in. He was a tall, handsome man, gentlemanly and friendly, greeting us politely whenever we met. To my father's uneasy questions he replied: 'You must understand that we Germans do not plan to harm you. We are civilized people.' We wanted so much to believe him, but they forced us to wear the yellow star of David sewn on to our clothing and disquieting rumours were spreading. We celebrated Pesach and tried to think of nothing else.

On Sunday 9 April, the last night of Pesach, came the decree: 'Pack your belongings, as much as you can carry, and be prepared to move. After seven in the morning no one is allowed on the streets, and when the police come you will accompany them to the room which has been assigned to you in the newly established ghetto.'

The feeling – that the world was about to end – which I had managed to keep at a distance – enveloped me afresh. We had no time for questions: we had to start packing. We would take our personal belongings, as much as we could carry, and each our own mattress, food and cooking-utensils. If one had access to a barrow, everything could be loaded onto that, otherwise one had to carry it oneself. Father went out to find a barrow, mother began to plan the food, I packed my books, and Livi played with the cat.

'We have no bread,' said mother.

'We shall have to manage without,' said father.

'No,' I said. 'I'll run out just before seven. I'll be back in time. Kira bakes early.' I knew that that baker always started work before the others.

'What will happen to us?' asked mother.

'We shall manage somehow,' said father. 'We've always managed somehow.'

Mother would not be calmed. 'Must we leave our home, our possessions?'

'It doesn't matter; we'll lock up when we go. It may not be for too long,' said father.

'But how shall we live in one small room?'

'Where shall we cook?'

'Where shall we wash?'

'We shall have to manage,' said father.

'Let us hope it will be a big, light room.'

'We shall see.'

We started to pack and went round the rooms taking farewell of our home and saying goodbye to the photographs hanging from the walls, our grandfathers and grandmothers. Mother began to cry.

'Why are you crying?'

'At leaving everything. Our home, our beautiful furniture, carpets, paintings. It's hard.'

'They're just objects. The important thing is that we keep together. What does it matter if we live in an empty hut as long as we can all be together?'

'You are right.'

'So why are you crying?'

'Everything has memories. How hard do you think your father had to work to buy this drawing-room furniture? We got them on our wedding anniversary. It was then he gave me that beautiful painting in the dining-room. We were so happy.'

I remembered. It was for that anniversary that I had embroidered a little gypsy tapestry as a surprise. It still hung in the dining-room. We would have to leave that too. And the ornaments, the little ballerina, the blue vase supported by two mermaids, grandfather's wall-clock. We were not rich, but my parents loved beautiful things. The house which they had so longed to buy and for which they had sacrificed so much, the first in the Functional style with a flat roof seen in Sighet. And our bathroom and flush closet, as uncommon as our running water. And the dining-room with its memories of simple family meals and wedding and birthday feasts, with guests from far away telling thrilling stories of the great world, and other occasions of joy and excitement.

I too went round the house to take farewell of familiar things. I did not feel the same bond to them as my mother, but looked sadly at the tiled stove, which radiated gentle warmth in winter, the soft couch where I would curl up with a book, and the glass cabinet, in which good things were always to be found: nut chocolate, toffees, candied fruit. My eyes ran along the walls and rested on the haystack in a painting, in which I always wanted to hide when things were bad. I would have liked to do so now.

I went to the piano and struck a few chords, to the bookcase and took out some books. Rimbaud, Villon, Géraldy, you can't come with me. Nor my beloved Hungarian poets, Ady and Arany. At that moment I swore a sacred oath: I shall never bind myself to objects; I shall never weep for material things; I shall never mourn the loss of anything that can be replaced by money. Yet I could not but mourn the jasmine bush in the garden, which sprouted nakedly to the blue spring sky. It was there I used to hide when I wanted to be alone; those flowers had comforted me when I was sad.

The spring sun peeped through the gap in the blinds, and I woke with a stab of pain. It was Monday morning and I must hurry to buy bread. Soon the police would come in their cock-feathered hats to fetch us. I threw on my clothes, ran to the bakery, bought bread and ran home again. On the way I met other people on the same errand. We scarcely exchanged greetings. Our minds were full.

Back at home we sat down at the breakfast table and tried to comfort each other. Mother was inconsolable, father tried to be practical, and my sister, at fourteen, was too young fully to understand. She was happy at what seemed to her an exciting adventure. I tried to be sensible, but my heart ached with premonitions. Was having to move the worst that could happen to us or merely the beginning of something much worse?

I hid my diaries under the roofbeam, together with my favourite books, and hoped I would soon be able to come back and collect them. We had already handed our valuables to our neighbour, Mrs Fekete, who had volunteered to hide them. She had visited us one day in March and told us that her husband, an officer in the

Hungarian Army, had heard that we were to be moved. She thought we would have difficulty in hiding our valuables; they should have been handed in to the authorities long ago. When a family was moved, the house would be searched, and if any valuables were found, severe punishment would follow. So she offered to help us and keep the jewels and everything until we came back. I kept only my thin necklace with its heart and clover, and the little pewter ring which my boyfriend Puiu had given me.

I went up to my room and looked round. This room that has been my home, that has seen me grow from a child to a teenager, that I must now leave, probably for ever. Even if I come back, I shall not be the same person. When I close the door of this room, it will be for ever.

It was a little attic room with two small windows. Through one window I looked out onto the garden, with my beloved jasmine bushes, apricot and walnut trees, and the kennel with faithful old Bodri. We could not take him with us. The other window gave on to our neighbours, where in an identical loft lived Geza, my first great love. How many times had I not sat in the window till late at night and whispered words of love to his shadow? Or just looked at the moon and sighed longingly.

The room was sparsely furnished. Two narrow beds, a table, four chairs and a bookshelf. Some pictures on the walls and a mirror, and in a corner an empty, gaping iron stove. There was no room for more, but the warm colours made the room far from spartan to the eye. My room was a part of me, yet it was only the books whose loss I mourned.

The hours crept slowly. Breakfast was finished; the dishes were washed. I kept running to the window to see if any waving cock-feathers were approaching. The evacuation was to begin in the town square, and we lived almost next to the railway station, so that it would be some hours before our turn came. Half of the 30,000 inhabitants of the town were Jews. The evacuation would take several days. The last newspaper arrived, and the last postal delivery. I went and stroked Bodri one last time. Everything I did was in the knowledge that it was for the last time.

Would we have time to eat lunch? Since the police had not yet come into sight, mother called to me to lay the table. We would prepare something that would not take long. Mother took some eggs and told me to bring the goose fat from the larder. The goose fat was kept in big jars; in the autumn mother would buy several geese and melt down the fat so that it would serve us for the whole winter. She was always insistent that we should use it sparingly. Goose fat was dear.

When I returned with a small spoonful, she looked at me and said: 'Go and get more. We needn't economize on fat today. We shall have to leave it all behind.'

I went and fetched more. Mother made scrambled eggs which tasted as never before.

'How much better they are if one doesn't have to be mean with the fat.'

We ate the scrambled eggs with the fresh bread and drank tea. We ate in silence but all had the same thoughts. Our last meal. When the police opened the gate, I went to the lavatory to pull the plug one last time.

The sound of the rushing water followed me as I walked into the kitchen and met the cock-feathers. They did not need to speak. Silently we gathered up our belongings and left the house. It was unpleasant to walk through the town with the cock-feathers behind us. Curious neighbours peeped from behind their curtains, not daring to come out. Not a single person registered sympathy. Yet we had lived side by side for all these years, shared our joys and sorrows.

After half an hour we reached the ghetto. It was the poor quarter of the town, and they had surrounded it with a fence after moving the Christian inhabitants out. We were allotted a small room in a hut which comprised two rooms and a kitchen. The other room was occupied by the original tenant, a poor widow with seven children.

We entered the yard and were met by the woman. She was wailing loudly. I recognized her as Aunt Marja, who helped us with our housework and laundry.

'Who could have imagined that fine people like you would be forced to live in my poor hut? Alas, alas!' she wailed, wringing her hands. 'That Hitler should have been burned alive. What will become of us? What will he think of next? He should be burned alive.'

'Calm yourself, Marja dear,' said father. 'Things will work out. We won't cause you any trouble; we'll keep to our room. I'm happy that we can live here with you.'

'You're no trouble,' said Marja. 'You can use my kitchen, and I shall help you with everything.'

'But we have no money to pay you,' said my mother.

'That doesn't matter. I don't want any money. You've always been good to me.'

While they talked, Livi and I looked at the dirty and snivelling children who were running in and out. We knew that Marja had many children but had never before seen any of them.

'You can play with my doll.' said one of the children who was about Livi's age. She had been watching Livi admiringly for some while before she dared to address her.

'I don't play with dolls any longer,' said Livi.

The girl looked at us in disappointment and went into the house. I saw another face behind the window, distrustful and contemptuous. Clearly the whole family was not as well disposed towards us as Aunt Marja.

Aunt Marja showed us round. In the middle of the stone-paved yard was the well. Water was pulled up in a bucket on a rope. Further off stood a shed; the stench from it showed it to be the lavatory. I shrank from the thought of using it. The yard led directly into the kitchen, which was small, disorderly, dark and filled with smoke. From the kitchen two doors led into the other rooms, one of which was to be ours. It smelled dank and was dirty and dark. A small room with two beds and a couch, a small table, two ribbed chairs and a cupboard. That was all the furniture, and there would hardly be room for more. A little iron stove sat glumly in one corner, and a mirror grinned crookedly from the wall.

'Where shall I sleep?' asked Livi.

'You and Hedi will have to sleep on the couch,' said mother.

'I can't sleep with her,' I shouted. 'She tosses and turns all night. And she snuffles. I shan't get a wink of sleep.'

'That can't be helped. Tomorrow I'll try to find another bed. Tonight you'll have to manage. Now we must start to clean the room up – we can't live like this. We'll have to scrub the floor and walls. There are sure to be lice.'

We began the cleaning, scrubbed and toiled, the smell of soap piercing our lungs and making us forget everything else. We scoured and scraped, shook the bedclothes, cleaned the windows, waxed the stove. By evening we were so tired that we hardly had the strength to eat the sandwiches we had brought from our home. After the meal we fell into bed, happy with the work we had done and enjoying the smell of our own clean sheets. I did not even notice that I was sleeping with Livi and dropped off before I could think about it.

Next day we went out to reconnoitre. The ghetto consisted of several blocks surrounded by the fence. Those windows that overlooked the main street outside were nailed fast and painted over. The single street within the ghetto was crowded with people greeting each other with wordless glances. They understood. I saw my friends Dora and Sussie talking with Anna. Baba approached from the other direction. We were happy to see each other and felt strengthened by the knowledge that we would be living so close together. We walked around and found a little stream behind the houses which we at once chose as our meeting-place. It felt good to have a refuge of our own.

Even before everyone had moved in, people began to organize life inside the fence – such things as ghetto police, public cleaning and care of the sick. Those Jews who were in hospital were sent to the ghetto and had to be put into proper care without delay. The ghetto began to buzz with activity. The synagogue, which was the only building empty, became the hospital. Beds and mattresses were procured, and soon patients dying of tuberculosis were lying side by side with those with broken legs, in the place where a few days earlier people had been praying and thanking Almighty God for having delivered our ancestors from Egypt.

The women were bedded in the women's gallery. There were no medicines or bandages. Sheets and curtains had to be cut up and used, washed, ironed and used again. The only pain-killer available was aspirin, and that had to be used sparingly. What we had plenty of was doctors – skilful and even famous ones. We girls volunteered as nurses, and that helped to pass the time.

Within a few days the whole Jewish population of the town had been gathered into the ghetto. Most of the houses contained ten or so families, two or three to each room. The entry to the ghetto was sealed and guarded by the cock-feathered police. No one was allowed to leave, and no one might enter, except the Hungarian camp commandant, who came every morning to receive a report from the Jewish elder responsible for seeing that official orders were carried out.

The days passed slowly. We began to get used to the crowding, but life was tense. The sisterly rivalry between Livi and me flared up again. We stood elbowing each other in front of the little mirror in our room. Each of us wanted to comb our hair, and each thought she had the right to the mirror. Neither of us would yield, and to assert my senior rights I hit her. She hit back, and soon we were engaged in a real fight. We clawed each other and pulled hair. We hated each other without realizing that our hatred ought to be directed elsewhere.

Spring was on the way. As we walked to our meetings by the stream, we could see that the grass was growing greener every day while the buds swelled on the lilac bushes. Small crocuses began to spread their drowsy smell. As we sat and let the spring come to us, we could almost forget that we were not there of our free will. But only for a moment; then we began to talk of boys and awoke to reality. Dora read out a letter from her boyfriend, who had been arrested for holding communist ideas and was in prison awaiting a trial whose outcome was predetermined. Baba told us about a letter someone had had from the Ukraine, where her boyfriend was. According to this letter the Jewish hospital there had been burned down and everyone inside it had perished. No one knew if it was an accident or a deliberate act.

The inhabitants of the ghetto were mostly women, children and old people. All men of working age had been sent to the front to serve the Hungarian troops in such matters as removing mines. They had to walk barefoot in the minefields in front of the advancing soldiers and find the mines with their toes. Many lost their lives there. Letters were rare and were received with trepidation.

Everyone was afraid for everyone else, and as soon as anyone had a letter, people would gather to share the recipient's joy or grief.

When Baba had finished, we sat silent, each of us lost in her own thoughts. All were buried in gloom. I thought of Puiu, of whom I had heard nothing for a long time. Could he have been in that hospital? At the same time, I was happy that father was at home and that I had no brothers to worry about.

What did worry me was that our money and food were running out. What would happen then? We had money with Mrs Fekete, our former neighbour; it was just a question of getting out and fetching it. I discussed this with the girls, and it transpired that Dora had the same problem. The only way to get out was by volunteering for outside work. Each morning the camp commandant asked for volunteers who were then taken into town under guard to help with clearance work. Our houses and apartments, which we had locked so carefully when we left, had not remained locked for long. As soon as we were in the ghetto, they were expropriated and handed over to German and Hungarian officers. But before the new owners moved in, they had to be emptied of all unnecessary rubbish'.

Dora and I went that afternoon to offer our services. We were accepted and told to be at the ghetto entrance next morning at eight. I went home and told my parents of my plan. I intended to slip away from my clearance work, go to Mrs Fekete and fetch some of the money we had left with her when she had offered to look after our jewels. Mother became uneasy and tried to dissuade me. I knew they had threatened to shoot us if we tried to meet anyone outside the ghetto, but I felt I had no choice. Father was likewise worried, but in the end they yielded, warning me to be careful.

I went to bed but found it difficult to sleep. I tried to plan my escape but it was impossible to guess in which part of the town we would be working. I hoped it would be near our house. Since the food situation in the ghetto was becoming critical, I also hoped that Mrs Fekete might take pity on us and let us have something. She had after all warned us that we would be sent away, although her husband was a Hungarian officer. In my imagination I saw piles of food, and decided to take a big coat with inside pockets to hide whatever she might give us. Or should I try to bribe the guard? Flour, sugar, butter, eggs … She might even give us a bottle of milk for our cousin's baby if I asked her. Everything in the ghetto was in short supply. The little store was beginning to run out of goods, and what was left was becoming ever more expensive. It was a long time since we had seen milk. But still there was food for those with money. The black-market sharks saw to that. Once I was outside the ghetto … Tomorrow.

As day dawned, I jumped out of bed, dressed, drank a cup of tea and ran off to fetch Dora. She met me at the door and we went together to the gate where three other girls were waiting. When we had been identified, the gate was opened and we were allowed to leave, guarded by three policemen. It was strange to see these familiar streets so quiet, instead of bubbling with life. We walked down the High Street. Only a few shops were open. Most of the shops in the town had been owned by Jews, and now their shutters were closed.

No Pista in front of Uncle Samuel's textile shop, busy sweeping the pavement. Pista was the errand boy, who used to sprinkle water through a funnel to lay the dust. He drew figures-of-eight with the falling water – we used to call him 'Water Eight'. Now he too was in the ghetto.

No Uncle Kaufman outside the bookshop, ready to open up. No Aunt Ilus in the sweetshop; she always gave us a twist of toffees. And no smell of lavender in front of Darvas's perfume shop. That was shut too.

The spring sun shone only on the Hungarian barber Kocsis, standing before the previously Jewish-owned shop waiting for customers. But no customers came. No men were walking to work, no women to the square with baskets on their arms. Scarcely any children or ownerless dogs. Even the cab-horses were gone – they too were owned by Jews. The policeman on the street corner looked dully into the distance, with nothing to do. I wondered what he was thinking about.

The town was buried in sleep, like the princess in the fairy tale. Would a prince ever come to kiss it to life again? I wanted to hope so.

Now we left the High Street and turned towards the station. A housewife was leaning out of the window shaking bedclothes. For her it was just another day – her man was at work, her children at school. She would have a good dinner prepared for their return, and none of them would think about us, their former neighbours. But most of the windows in the houses gaped empty, their blinds drawn, houses whose owners were, like us, in the ghetto.

We stopped at a small villa not far from where the Feketes lived and were ordered to sort the contents and make an inventory: furniture in one pile, china in another, clothes in a third, ornaments in a fourth. What would be done with it all we did not know, though I assumed that it would be taken to Germany. Anything that was worth anything.

It was horrible to root around in other people's homes, emptying drawers of photographs into the dustbins, photographs that meant so much to those who had owned them. I began to feel sick and was glad that I did not know any of the people who had lived there. It was hard to imagine that the same thing was happening in our home, that someone was sorting everything that we had owned and cherished into despised heaps. Yet it felt good to be outside the ghetto and doing a job, even this.

All the time I was watching for an opportunity to run off to Mrs Fekete. The hours passed, the clock struck one, and soon we would return to the ghetto. I plucked up my courage, went to the guard, told him I had left a love-token at home and asked if I might retrieve it. I was lucky – he proved sympathetic and promised to turn a blind eye for a moment if I was quick. I ran off and within a few minutes was standing at Mrs Fekete's gate. Before I rang the bell, I looked furtively at the house next door, where, not so long ago, we had lived. Only the window of the drawing-room, where the German officer lived, was open. The blinds on the other windows were still drawn. Evidently nobody else had yet moved in.

I rang Mrs Fekete's bell. She opened the door. When she saw me, she stiffened.

'What are you doing here?'

'I need a little money.'

'I have no money. Why should I give you money?'

'But we left a lot of money with you before we went away.'

'What money? I haven't had any money from you. You'd best be off before my husband returns. If he finds you here, it'll be the worse for you.'

There was nothing to do but turn and go. I ran back, my heart in my shoes. I had not expected this. Now I understood why she had been so 'nice', this Hungarian officer's wife who had secretly warned us. I should have guessed she had such a motive. Why not get something out of the Jews, since everyone else was? We were still naïve. How long would it be before we dared to look truth in the face?

I was ashamed as I walked back through the ghetto

gate. My plan had failed. But once inside I was greeted by news which almost made me forget it. The men, apart from those who had died in the Ukraine, were back. There was great excitement and joy at seeing them, but uncertainty and worry as to what it might signify. Was it a good sign, or bad? The boys joined us by the stream, and we tried to solve the riddle together. In the end we agreed that it must be a good sign, or anyway not too bad. The rumour spread that we would be sent to do agricultural work, and if so, it was natural that the men would be required first. This riddle solved, we rejoiced at having our boyfriends back and our debates by the stream enhanced by their views. We wanted to hear everything that had happened to them, and they wanted to hear how things had been with us. We met by the stream morning, noon and night, we had so much to talk about. We did not care that it was forbidden to be outside after six, for we had discovered secret ways home.

What did we talk about? Mostly the situation in the ghetto, the daily problems, the hopelessness and possible solutions – which we then rejected as impossible. The war came closer, and our discussions usually ended: 'They won't be able to do much more. The Soviets will soon be here.' Then we passed on to books, singing songs and surrendering ourselves to thoughts of love, which even the Germans could not frighten away from our young hearts.

Only one man stood silent and serious, a little to one side. He seldom joined in the conversation, was not really one of us. This was Michael, with the big, sad eyes and intense personality, whom I had seen several times since the men returned. He was much older than I and was not interested in the young girl who looked admiringly at him. That he would later become my husband none of us could have guessed.

Michael was one of the few who dared to see the situation as it was. He knew that the rumours were true and was determined not to sit and wait, but to do something. He did not want to be there when we were collected to be taken to 'work in the fields', even if that meant going to the heart of Hungary. He was planning to escape up into the mountains and wait there for the Soviets. He knew the forests well and was sure he could hide from the police. He would take food in a haversack, and even if the Soviets were a hundred kilometres away, he would rather take the risk than let himself be transported to no-one-knew-where.

All this I heard later from his mother, when she told us in tears of her son's venture. My mother tried to console her, but it was difficult. Her husband had died shortly before we were brought to the ghetto, and now she was alone. She wept, and my mother wept with her. It was a common sight, weeping women; it gave them at least momentary relief. We young people despised their weakness. We felt strong. Our camaraderie and innocence gave us strength. We cheered each other up and tried to do the same for our parents. But I felt a lump in my chest, a foreboding of something terrible. In my head I could accept that 'everything will be all right', and 'the Soviets will soon be here', but not in my heart.

At last, on 14 May, the order was issued: tomorrow the transports will leave, starting with our street and continuing until the ghetto is empty. Where to? To the interior of Hungary, to do agricultural work. We all looked at each other. Everyone was afraid. Stories of camps, of cruelties, began to spread. But I felt only an inexpressible relief. For a month we had lived in the ghetto, uncertain what would happen. Each morning we had woken uneasily: what would the day hold for us? And each night we fell asleep with the same unease. To what will we awaken? What is going to happen? Now that I at last knew what was to happen, I felt relieved, almost elated. Uncertainty is always the hardest thing to bear.

I hugged my mother and said: 'Don't worry. I feel everything is going to be all right.'

'Do you think so?' asked mother, a glimmer of hope in her sad eyes.

'I'm sure of it. They're tired of having us here doing nothing day after day and being no use to them. It is spring, the men are at the front, they need help in the fields. We shall get food, perhaps even a little money.'

'Let us hope you are right,' said mother, and went to discuss the situation with her neighbours.

Naturally no one wanted to believe otherwise. Mother was quick to tell them what I had said, and most people were willing to believe me. But some had other things to say:

'We won't be taken anywhere. The Soviets are only ten kilometres from here – they'll be here before dawn,' said Mrs Weiss, who was always well-informed.

'Then we'll be able to go back to our homes,' said Mrs Grün, and hurried back to her family to pass on the good news.

'Can one be sure of that?' asked a third doubtfully.

'Even if the Soviets don't arrive and they take us away, that can't be so dangerous. Why must people always expect the worst? Hedi is right: they need our work. We shall be taken to the fields.'

'But suppose they want to harm us?' asked Moshe, who was notorious for always looking on the dark side of things.

'Don't be such a pessimist,' replied Eli. 'We aren't living in the Middle Ages. We're living in a civilized world. Why should they want to harm us? We haven't hurt anyone.'

That was logical. People began to feel calmer. But

someone turned to Mrs Weiss and asked: 'How do you know the Soviets are so near?'

'I heard it from Mrs Kohn, who had it from her husband, who is a good friend of Istvan, the policeman.'

'Where do you think he got it from?'

'The police must know. They hear things from their officers.'

'Then our trials are over. Tomorrow we shall go home. I always knew the Soviets would be our saviours. He's good, that Stalin.'

So easy it is to lull oneself into a false sense of hope. The smallest straw we accepted gratefully.

That night I did not sleep. I was on duty at the temporary hospital. On the rickety, crowded beds lay groaning men and women, who had not yet heard about the transports. There was no point in telling them. It was best to stay silent. I put on my white coat, which I still had from my schooldays, and went into the hall. I walked round, took temperatures and saw that everything was as it should be for the night. Uncle Salman, a nice old man whom I remembered from my childhood, groaned and turned uneasily in his bed.

'Can I have a little water? I'm in such pain.'

He had advanced cancer and knew we had no pain-killers. But he could have a little water. I gave him some, bathed his forehead and sat beside his bed. He lifted his eyes gratefully and tried to smile. I was ashamed not to be able to do more for him, and stroked his bony hand. I looked at the pale, sunken face. The parchment-like skin was transparent, the purplish veins visible beneath it. It was the face of a human being on his way to the other side. I remembered him in his prime, when he came driving his horse-drawn cab, jesting merrily. In the summers he would drive us to the river to bathe, in the winters to places where we could toboggan. The bells on his cab rang softly, and we children, huddled in our warm furs, listened breathlessly to his stories. He always had a tale for us, or a joke, and I could still hear his noisy laugh. Now his laughter was gone. What will become of him? And all the other old people in the hospital? Will they be left here, and if so, who will look after them? Or must we take them with us? How will they survive a journey? Will they survive here in the ghetto hospital? No, not even if people stay to look after them.

Things were already hard: we had no medicines, no bandages, no pain-killers. We had hardly any food. For some time the elders of the ghetto had begged the commandant for necessities, but they had scarcely been able to buy even the most basic commodities. And money was beginning to run out – one had to barter what valuables one had left in order to eat. And we had few of them, for the police carried out regular searches to discover what we had hidden.

While I sat there and let my thoughts wander, Salman fell asleep. I got up quietly and, after stroking his hand once more, went on to little Jonas's bed. He was eight and had a broken leg.

'How does it feel, Jonas?'

'Good.'

'Doesn't it hurt any longer?'

'Only a little.'

'Tomorrow we'll remove the plaster of Paris, and then you'll be out and able to run again. But remember, you mustn't see whether you or Bandi can jump furthest from the cellar roof. You don't want to come back here, do you?'

'No, I promise I won't.'

Nice that he'll go home to his mother before they take us away. I mustn't forget to tell Vera she must take off the plaster very early. And I must visit Jonas's mother before I go home and ask her to fetch him before seven.

I tucked the child up. He had fallen asleep with a smile on his lips, in happy confidence that tomorrow all the pain would be gone.

I looked round the hall. Most people had fallen asleep. I put out the light and went into the 'office', a small cubby-hole which had formerly been used as a lumber-room. There sat my dejected colleagues, still discussing the latest order. I told them what I thought: agricultural work in the interior. Most of them were willing to believe it.

Our conversation was interrupted by the entry of Peter, Magda's husband. Magda had been a classmate of mine and had married the previous year. When she was barred from going into the sixth form, her parents found a suitable young man and married her to him. I knew she was heavily pregnant, so I was not surprised when Peter told us that her labour had begun. I went out to receive her and put her in a bed in the gallery. She would have to bear her child among the other sick women, but I managed to find a screen which gave her a little privacy. Magda was in a confused state, happy yet worried, and I tried to calm her. I helped her wash and sat with her. Peter went home; there was nothing he could do. Before he left, I had to promise him I would go myself to tell him as soon as the baby was born.

Magda was worried about the journey. How would she be able to look after a new-born baby in the conditions which must be expected? I did not dare say much. I was worried for her. But when her pains began, we both forgot what lay ahead and thought only of the delivery. I ran for the midwife. She examined Magda, found everything in order and left us. It was not long before the labour began again and Magda began to shriek. I was unsure what to do and ran again to the midwife.

'Quick, do something. Help her! She's in pain,' I said.

'There's nothing I can do,' she replied reassuringly. 'Everything's as it should be. It is painful to bear children, but it isn't dangerous.'

It was the first time I had seen a birth. Is this how one has a child? Will she die? Stories of women who died in childbirth pass through my mind. I don't think I shall ever want to have any children if it is this difficult. But suddenly a harsh scream, and a sticky dark ball tumbled out between Magda's legs. The midwife snipped the umbilical cord and smacked the baby's bottom several times. There was a weak squawk.

'A boy, Magda! You've got a boy!' I cried. 'He's dark. Look, Magda, look!'

With a pale smile she looked at the child and passively allowed us to knead her to get rid of the afterbirth. The next moment she was asleep. My heart sang. Life is not over. We shall be taken away tomorrow, but we have with us a new life which will continue after we are gone.

The midwife washed the baby, wrapped him in some clean strips of sheet and laid him beside Magda. I sat down on a chair by the bed and could not stop looking at him. Dawn peered in through the window. Magda and the baby were still asleep. Suddenly I remembered Peter, Jonas and everything else. I took off my white coat and went to Peter. I did not need to wake him. He sat smoking nervously, a full ashtray and an empty coffee cup in front of him. When he heard the news, he gave a shout of joy, lifted me up and swung me round in the air.

'He shall be called Nathaniel, "the one given by God"!'

He put me down and ran to the hospital.

Jonas's parents were already up when I called, about to leave for the hospital. They had decided to bring him home and were pleased to know that the plaster would be off when they arrived. Then I went home.

Mother and father were busy putting together our

belongings. We had to be outside with them by seven. None of us might carry more than twenty kilos; everything else we must leave behind in the ghetto. Now my rucksack came in useful, the one I had made before we were taken from home. I packed some dresses, a few underclothes, extra shoes and stockings, a jumper, two books, writing-materials, and a small bag containing a change of underclothes, stockings and my diary, in case the rucksack proved too heavy and had to be left behind.

Now I remembered my dream. The nightmare which had perhaps been the reason why I had made the rucksack. The eternally wandering procession of men and women with sacks on their backs and staffs in their hands, sometimes on the highway, sometimes on forest paths, sometimes alongside ditches, sometimes by rivers. Mother's dream or my dream. Can one inherit dreams? Is it the collective unconscious? Will my grandchildren dream the same dream?

When I went out to the street, things were still quiet, but seven o'clock was approaching and people began to leave their houses. Suddenly I saw Michael.

'You here? What has happened? You were going to hide in the mountains,' I cried, without thinking that we had never previously exchanged a word.

'I tried. Feri and I went up to Pietrosul, up above where we used to make excursions, you know. We thought we would be safe there – the forests are deep, and we know every nook of them. But we were unlucky. A Ruthenian shepherd looking for a lost sheep evidently spotted us. We were just wondering if he'd seen us when our cock-feathered friends arrived. Those Ruthenian farmers have never liked us Jews.'

'What did the police do?'

'The awful thing is that they did nothing. Just handcuffed us and ordered us to go with them. Naturally we thought they would take us to prison. But they brought us back here to the ghetto. That means that the fate which awaits us here will not be lighter than the punishment we would have got for running away.'

'What do you think does await us?'

'Nothing good, that's sure. Not work in the fields of Hungary.'

While we talked, several people had gathered round to listen, and now someone began to wail. But there was no time for further guesses or words of consolation. It was getting late, and noisier by the minute. Those still indoors shouted to those outside and vice versa. People came with their sacks, bags, bundles, rucksacks, parcels in brown wrapping-paper and elegant suitcases. Some had put on their best clothes, some wore two of everything. Our family had decided that we should wear light sporting clothes. I had on slacks, a blouse, a jumper, a jacket and boots, and stared in amazement at women in high-heeled shoes. People ran out of the houses and back in – here was something forgotten, there something else that had to be taken along. Someone wanted help, someone else wanted something else, and suddenly the whole street had become a beehive full of seemingly haphazard rushing and buzzing. Small children cried, dogs barked.

The cock-feathered police arrived and ordered us to line up in front of the houses by families in ranks of five. At first they tried to arrange things peacefully, but it was difficult, terrified and undisciplined as we were, to get us to obey. Then they began to shout and threatened us with rifles. But the people would not calm down. Shouts, screams and weeping mingled with the barking of the dogs and the coarse oaths of the police. Suddenly a shot rang out and there was silence. A proclamation was read out:

1. The ghetto is to be evacuated. All Jews will be

removed to the Hungarian interior.

2. No person may carry more than twenty kilos.
3. All valuables shall immediately be handed to the police.
4. Any person found with valuables in his or her possession will be shot immediately.
5. Any person attempting to escape will be shot.

When the reading was finished, the people began to buzz and rush around again, and the cock-feathers tried in vain to get the 3,000 from our street into some kind of order. I stood obediently in front of our house and was glad that the evacuation was to begin with our street. We were being taken away, and this was better than that eternal speculation. Soon we would know what awaited us at the end of the journey, and knowledge at least dispels uncertainty. Gradually the people became calm, stood in ordered lines and waited.

We stood in the street for hour after hour. It was not easy to keep the children quiet. The adults became restless, some grew thirsty, some wanted to relieve themselves, but nobody was allowed to move. The crowd of people, with the yellow star shining on every breast, rumbled in increasing agitation. When the rumbling began to sound threatening, several shots were fired in the air. These had some effect for a while.

What were we waiting for? No one knew. We must have waited for several hours, for the sun was high in the heaven when the signal for our departure was given and we moved out of the ghetto.

We were taken to the great synagogue in the town. There the families were divided, the men crammed into the main hall, the women and children into the gallery. We were used to sitting apart from our men in the synagogue, so this did not especially bother us. But we suffered from overcrowding and thirst. The cock-feathers began to go through our belongings, looking for valuables. They called the women one by one, and female guards body-searched us in case we were hiding anything in our orifices.

We sat on the benches. The men wrapped themselves in their prayer shawls and prayed. Many women took out their prayer books, while others tried to comfort each other with hopeful rumours:

'The Soviets are only ten kilometres away,' repeated Mrs Weiss, she who was always so well informed. 'If you listen hard, you can hear the guns.'

'You said that several weeks ago,' someone replied.

'But now it is true. They're very close.'

'But who says they'll be here by morning?'

'Yes, they will. God holds His protecting hand over us.'

'Are we not sitting in the synagogue praying? Do you think God doesn't listen?'

'You're lucky if you believe that.'

'You'll see, the Soviets will be here before dawn, and we'll be able to go home again.'

'Home to the ghetto?'

'No, home to our houses. We shall breakfast in our old homes.'

Even the unconfident allowed themselves to be comforted, they so wanted to believe it.

The rumour spread from the gallery to the men below. By the time it had returned to us, the proximity of the Soviets had been reduced by several kilometres. As time passed, people began to speak of shots heard from the outskirts of town. Thus was sustained the courage of the tired and frozen.

We were not allowed to leave the synagogue, even to visit the toilet. The stink and thirst became intolerable; children cried, women fainted. I determined to get a little water and went to the door to speak with the police. Being a well-brought-up girl, I asked politely to be allowed to fetch some water. A contemptuous glance and a harsh 'No' were the answer. I was frightened the policeman would hit me and moved aside.

After a moment Anna came and talked to the same policeman. She apologized for his having to waste such a beautiful evening looking after us, and babbled on until they had become involved in a lively conversation. They joked and laughed; then Anna turned to him with a seductive glance and a voice that brooked no opposition: 'I'll just get a drink of water.' And she went.

I stared uncomprehendingly. It was no use being well brought up. If you pleaded and made yourself small, you just got kicked. One had to be bold, assert oneself, earn respect. I suddenly realized that the childhood formula 'You shall have it if you're good' was only a trick by adults to get children to obey, resulting in our conviction that, 'They won't hurt us if we're good, if we co-operate, if we do as they say.'

Day darkened into evening, evening into night, and we sat on, alternating between fear and hope. Dawn came but no Soviets. We were formed up again and marched to the station.

15 May 1944

It was a grey dawn. The rosy clouds, harbingers of the sun, promised a fine day. We dragged our tired limbs along, our bags feeling heavier and heavier with every step we took. Anyone who fell out of line received a blow on the head from a stick. Families held each other by the hand; they wanted to keep together. More and more people threw aside their sacks to help those who could not manage. As we marched down the streets, the sun rose over the housetops, and by the time we reached the park, it was touching the newly emerged leaves, the budding tulips and the small carpet of crocuses. All was silent. The little town was asleep. The church clock struck six as we passed. They had calculated well. No one would see us as we were led away.

When the people awake, they will draw their blinds and say: 'What a wonderful day!'

I looked around, to say goodbye to my little town. To the park with the little pavilion, where the military band used to play on Sundays. Where I used to walk in the hope of meeting the Someone with whom I was in love just then. Where I used to sit with my friends and philosophize about life, mankind and love. To my school, Domnita Ileana, where I had studied for seven years, rejoiced in new knowledge and grieved over failures. To Uncle Samuel's textile shop, where we would meet just before closing-time to arrange little parties. To the cinema, which pupils were forbidden to enter but which we would slip into on Sunday afternoons, hiding under the seats in the interval. To the café, which had the best Dobos cake in the world and where loving couples could hide in the alcoves along the walls. I loved their Froufrou, a chestnut mousse with whipped cream – shall I ever taste that again?

A thin dog stood on the street corner and turned its scabby head after us as though wishing to say goodbye. The dog's sad eyes increased my sadness and remained with me long afterwards.

The station. We had arrived. Now I don't remember the sun any longer – can it have gone behind the clouds? Freight wagons stood before us, their windows nailed up. These were for us. A hundred of us were pushed into each wagon, which normally held eight horses. We were tired, hungry, thirsty and rather apathetic. We allowed ourselves to be shoved in, saw the policemen lock the doors and heard them shoot the heavy metal bolts. Now it was really dark, with only a weak light filtering in. We sat down as best we could and talked softly.

Now, for the first time, I looked around to see who was with us. I knew most of them, but none of my best friends was there. People sat dumbly. Those who had food took it out and tried to eat. Someone began to dole out the water which had been handed in before the doors were closed. A place was decided on for the excrement bucket, and someone tried to hang a blanket in front of it. The train bumped on the stone chippings, and we began to discuss what it all might mean. We still hoped we might be taken to the Hungarian interior.

'How old do you think I should say I am?' asked father. 'I shall be fifty in July. Perhaps they will not make me work if I say I am over fifty.'

My intuition told me that this would be a bad tactic: 'I think it would be best if you say you are younger. It'll surely be better if we can all work. You can manage, and mother is young. And Livi is almost grown up.'

'But suppose we get taken somewhere else?'

'We must get work, wherever we go. Why else should they be moving us?'

But slowly suspicions began to arise. Or was it that now people began to clothe their fears in words? Now, when there was no longer any turning back. Do they intend to kill us? Are they taking us to some uninhabited place to shoot us? Will they pump poison gas into the waggons? My mother remembered that the Polish refugee had told of waggonloads of people who had been murdered in this way. I listened to the conversation and weighed the various possibilities. I heard voices within me. The poet Jozsef Attila wrote, in one of his finest lines: 'I have lived, and a person can die of living.' I too have lived. But something in me asked: Have I really lived? My other favourite poet, Arany, now replied: 'People may not die until they have been happy.' Have I been happy? I was a happy child, but I have not yet been a happy adult. I must not die. Perhaps I shall escape death. Perhaps we shall be taken to the Hungarian interior. As soon as we approached a station I tried to peep out through the slots in the window. As long as I could see Hungarian names, I felt comparatively safe.

I looked round at my companions. The families sat in tight groups as though protective of their territory. It was important to defend one's jealously acquired space from intruders who wanted to lie down or stretch their legs. Invisible walls began to rise, families behaved as though they were alone. Someone took out his food and began to eat, without the usual polite offer to his neighbour: 'Would you like some?' One family had discovered that something had been left behind, and they began to blame each other. A young couple sat caressing each other with an equal absence of embarrassment, while someone else performed his needs in the bucket.

The Grün family sat eating a ham they had brought. They were not orthodox; only the old grandmother remained Kosher. Normally they would have hidden their ham, but today they did not bother. The grandmother sat silent, buried in her thoughts, her tears two unending rivulets. Suddenly she looked up and said: 'Give me some ham. In my seventy-six years I have never eaten non-Kosher food, but now I intend to. If God can do this to us, I shall cease to obey His commandments.'

Everyone looked at her in dismay as she cut a slice and began to chew it meditatively, as though awaiting an answer from God. She had not stopped believing in God; she just wanted to challenge Him. Perhaps she was hoping for a thunderbolt which would put an end to her miseries.

A little further off sat the Schwarz family, the mother, father, grandmother and three children. The smallest was only five. He sat on his grandmother's knee and asked her to tell him a story. The grandmother began to tell the story of Hansel and Gretel but clearly felt disturbed by the other family quarrelling beside her. She stopped, looked around and said: 'Come, little one, let's go to another room. There are too many people here.'

The child looked at her. 'But grandma, we're on the train. Don't you see?'

'Yes, but let us go into another room,' she said and made as though to move.

'Grandma, grandma, don't you see that we aren't at home? Don't you remember they locked us in the train? There are no rooms here.'

'We can go into the kitchen,' replied the grandmother, and looked into the distance with dead eyes.

'There isn't any kitchen here,' said the child, and pulled his grandmother's blouse to make her sit down again.

Several of those seated around tried to make the old lady understand, but she looked in bewilderment at these people who were trying to hinder her. Only when her daughter put her arms round her did she calm herself and agree to sit down again. The frightened gaze of the child did not leave the old lady's face. He dared not ask her to go on with the story. Grandmother was already far away and with the movements of one rocking a child began to sing old Jewish cradle-songs. Perhaps she believed she was back in her childhood home, rocking her small brother or sister, or perhaps her daughter?

3   Auschwitz

Night followed day, and day night. We tried to sleep sitting up; there was no room for us all to stretch out. At night we took turns to lie down for a short while. The bucket in the corner began to overflow, and the smell of sweat, urine and excrement was nauseating. Our supply of water ran out, and thirst became unbearable. People began to beg and pray, wail and shriek. When the train stopped, I tried to ask the guards for a little air and a little water, but in vain. We taught one of the small children some German phrases, lifted him to the window and got him to say: '*Bitte schön, Wasser*', but his tiny voice rang out unheard. The guards merely shouted at us to be quiet and threatened us with their rifles.

The station names ceased to be Hungarian. The train had changed direction and was no longer travelling westward. The names were Polish. Where were we going? Now we were prepared for the worst, but tiredness and thirst made us want to have everything behind us. If we were to die, let it happen soon; it could not be worse than this. The children cried. A girl fainted. Her mother began to scream for help, her father tried to rouse her. Water, water! Will no one have pity on us?

The train's whistle sounded, the train restarted, the journey continued. More hours passed. It became dark. Then the train halted in a siding. The night was dark around us. Where were we? Those who were crowded closest to the window-cracks could make out a sign a little way off: Oświęcim. That told us nothing. People groaned, wept and prayed. Most were apathetic. The one thought uppermost in every mind was: WATER.

Mother sniffed the night air and thought she smelt something strange.

'I smell gas. Well, now it will happen. They're going to pump gas into the waggons,' she said, exhausted.

'No, mother, that isn't possible. We aren't sealed in. Air would get in through the cracks.'

'Don't you feel this overpowering smell?'

'It may be from the factory where we're going to work,' said father.

'Don't cry, mother,' said Livi. 'I'll help you to wash up every day.'

Mother stroked Livi and tried to smile.

Searchlights shone through the cracks, and after several hours the doors were opened. Grim men in striped clothes hunted us out of the waggons:

'*Raus, raus! Schnell, schnell!* Out, out! Quick, quick!' they shouted, swearing.

Everyone hurried to the exit, but my father and I stopped to ask one of the men: 'Where are we?'

The man in prison dress looked nervously around and, having assured himself that no one was listening, replied softly:

'Extermination camp.'

So at last we knew. We looked at each other but had no time to say anything.

'*Schnell, schnell! Macht dass ihr rauskommt, Sauschweine,*' roared the SS men who were watching the scene with their dogs from the platform. At regular intervals they cracked their whips and aimed a blow at any laggard.

A loudspeaker ordered: 'Men to the left, women to the

right,' and the truncheons ensured that the order was obeyed. I gave my father a quick kiss and told him to hurry so as not to be hit. After I had taken a few steps, I heard the crack of a whip and a cry. Was it my father? I shall never know.

I caught up with my mother and sister and joined the line. The long queue of women moved slowly towards a table where the SS man with his bloodhound was waving his stick like a conductor on his dais: 'You right, you left, right, left, left, left.' It was Wotan himself, ruling over life and death.

'We belong together. We want to stay together,' protested the families.

He looked passively in front of him and repeated mechanically: 'You will meet later. The old people and children will go by van. You are all going to the same place.'

Mothers reluctantly let go of their daughters; sisters parted from sisters.

Mother was inconsolable. As we wound forward in the long queue, Livi and I held her arm, and I tried to think of something to stop her crying.

'Mother, don't you think you have had a fine life?'

'I have. But you two, you haven't lived yet. Why must you die?'

'Don't think about it. Never mind about us. I don't mind that I must die.'

I accepted that we were being taken to our death. I accepted it calmly, without rebelling, without even thinking of resisting. Perhaps because in my inmost being I still could not believe it.

We had reached the tall blond SS man in his spotless uniform. Later I learned that his name was Dr Mengele. He raised his piercing eyes towards us and pointed to mother with his cane:

'You to the left, you two to the right.'

Mother, with her dark blue shawl over her head and her reddened eyes, clung tightly to us.

'They are my children.'

'You will meet them tomorrow.'

'Can I have a little water?'

'You will have coffee when you get there.'

Poor mother. She had no coffee when she got there. It was the gas tap that opened when she stood there and raised her thirsty lips to the spray.

I let go of her quickly. A little too quickly. In a fraction of a second the thought shot through my head: 'She is going to die, we shall live. I don't want to go with her. I want to live.'

As soon as we parted, my tears came. I was seized with a feeling of guilt. Suddenly I saw my young mother through the SS man's eyes. She looked old in the dark shawl with her reddened eyes. Why had I not made her stop crying? Why had I not taken off her shawl? Why? Why?

Livi could not understand why I was crying. I don't know what she felt, but she thought I had no reason to cry.

'Mother, mother, what will happen to mother?' I repeated again and again.

'You heard: she's going by van. She'll be there waiting for us.'

'I'm afraid she won't,' I said, but I didn't want to tell Livi what I had heard from the man at the train: 'Extermination camp.'

'Then we'll meet tomorrow,' said Livi.

But I knew better. And my conscience gave me no peace: it is my fault that she will die. I have cheated her. I shall live.

Unable to think of anything else, I followed the group,

which was lined up in ranks of five. We marched towards the camp and eventually came to a place with several barracks, which we were told were bath-houses. It was still dark, but there were searchlights here too. The SS man gave the order:

'Put all your belongings in one pile. If you have any money or valuables, give them to the woman at the desk. Anyone found in possession of valuables will be severely punished. Then undress. Pile your clothes neatly. Tie your shoes together, and put them in another pile.'

I did not understand how I would be able to find my clothes in so huge a pile but did as I was told. Obedience before all. I still had the little pewter ring that was a memento from Puiu. I also had my thin gold necklace with the heart, which I wanted never to be parted from. I went up to the woman, showed her the worthless ring and asked: 'May I keep this?'

She pulled the ring from me and threw it into a heap of rubbish. I looked at it and thought: 'If I can't keep a worthless memento, there's no point in keeping the necklace either,' and threw it onto the same rubbish-heap.

We stripped ourselves naked and lined up before a man who cut off all our hair. We tried to hide our nakedness with our hands, but the SS guards went round and beat anyone who was not standing upright. My time came. I swallowed, tried to forget where I was and stood to attention before the 'barber'. He stood on a stool, swung his scissors and ripped off all my hair, everything. First with the scissors, then with a machine. First my head, then under my arms and lastly between my thighs. He was not interested in my eyebrows.

After the haircut we were given small, evil-smelling pieces of soap and ordered to take a shower. After the shower we had to put on grey prison clothes, without having dried ourselves. It felt unpleasant but it had to be.

We could keep our own shoes, so we had to retrieve them from the pile. My comfortable black boots felt good, and I was sorry for all those girls who were now wobbling around on their elegant pumps.

When we were ready, we did not know each other. In the grey dawn there rocked a sea of grey billiard balls. I took Livi by the hand. I was frightened of losing her, frightened of not recognizing her if I did lose her. I looked at her. Her lovely raven plaits gone, my little sister had been changed into a boy. I looked at the others, trying to catch their eyes so that I might recognize my old friends. Suddenly I saw a Greek god raise his eyes. It was Dora. I had always admired her profile, but now, without hair, with her straight nose and regular features, she looked exactly like a statue by Phidias. Her eyes sought mine, and I saw doubt, then hesitant recognition.

'Hedi, is it you?'

'Don't you recognize me?'

'Yes. But we all look a bit strange.'

'Not you. You're beautiful even without hair,' I said, wondering how I looked. Probably only my big nose was visible now that I had no hair to hide behind. I felt my skull and shuddered. The touch was horrible.

The night had imperceptibly turned to dawn, the dawn to morning. The shivering mass of girls, more like a crowd of boys, crowded fearfully outside the bath-house. Again we had to form into a line, and our first roll-call began. I was last in the line and heard the SS man count carefully: 421. So that was all that was left of us, 421 women. And how many men? Perhaps the same number. Less than a third of the 3,000 who had left the ghetto on the morning of 15 May.

My reflections were interrupted by something wet touching my skull. I felt it; it was a raindrop. Several soon followed. I felt them roll down my skull and be caught in my eyebrows or form rivulets down my neck. I shivered, looked at the others and burst into laughter. My unfortunate drenched companions looked like newborn calves, grey, bald and unsteady on their feet, but there were no cows near to nuzzle up to. We had to stand in the rain while our guards went into their hut. We waited outside without knowing what we were waiting for. The rain whipped our backs.

The day was far advanced when the SS commandant arrived who was to take charge of the 421 prisoners. He counted us once more, then gave the signal for us to march off.

On the way, behind a fence, we saw a group of women who we thought looked older. The girls began to shout and ask after our mothers, but they were told to be quiet and that it was forbidden to talk to fellow prisoners. The women looked at us curiously, without replying, but for the girls there was a glimmer of hope that our mothers might be among them. Why not? There was a camp for women, a camp for men, why should there not be a camp for old people and children? But I found it difficult to believe this, however hard the others tried to convince me.

We approached an area with low, scattered barracks, which could have been a factory but for the tall barbed-wire fence surrounding it, with the warning sign: THIS FENCE IS ELECTRIFIED. As far as the eye could see, the place was cold and sterile. No green anywhere. Not even a blade of grass. Even the sky was grey. Ever-swelling clouds of smoke blotted out the blue which we knew lay behind.

We were taken into one of the barracks. After the bright daylight, we were met by darkness. It took a moment before our eyes became accustomed to the light filtering in through two small windows at the end. The roof was low and by the door was a little alcove, the guard-room, where, as we later learned, the *blockova* – the woman in charge of the block – had her room. From it ran a narrow corridor to the left, with recesses on either side containing beds. These recesses were divided vertically, and on either side were three tiers of bunks measuring about three metres by two, leaving just enough headroom for people to sit upright on them. On each bunk ten girls would have to live, eat and sleep.

I and the nine nearest to me installed ourselves in one of the top bunks. It was rather a tight squeeze. When night came, it became clear that we had to lie head-to-feet. If anyone wanted to turn over, all the other nine had to do the same simultaneously. Any attempt to lie on one's back immediately evoked loud abuse. How many nights did I not lie on my side and dream of being able to stretch out on my back! Or curling up like a foetus – a luxury we could not allow ourselves.

We lay on bare boards with our shoes as a pillow. The girls on the bottom bunk lay on the floor, exposed to kicks from anyone who passed. Those on the middle bunk were disturbed repeatedly by the traffic from above, so I was happy to be on the top.

Five of us had kept together since we had been ordered to form lines of that number. Dora, beautiful, talented Dora, whom everyone looked up to, and I, together felt responsible for the children, Sussie, Livi and Ilu. Sussie, my cousin, was fifteen, Livi fourteen and Ilu, Sussie's cousin, twelve. Ilu was big for her age but was really only a child. She was the youngest of those who had entered Auschwitz, and you could tell it. She was very silent and withdrawn, had difficulty in learning to live without her parents and was apathetic, in contrast to the other two, who spent most of the time chattering. Sussie and Livi had long been close friends, as had Dora and I. Moreover, Dora was engaged to Tzali, Sussie's brother, who was in a

Romanian prison. All these bonds made us feel especially close and gave us a sense of double responsibility for each other.

When we had got up into the bunk, I could not help telling the others what I had heard on the train. They would not believe me. Dora listened thoughtfully, but Sussie and Livi went on happily babbling about how lovely it would be to see their mothers again. Eventually we fell asleep, exhausted.

Our awakening next morning was bitter. We remembered our mothers; I wept and could see nothing but her before my eyes. I thought also of father but did not grieve for him as I felt he must be alive somewhere in Auschwitz. I felt neither hunger nor thirst, and when our first meal was handed out, I gave my bread ration to Livi. I could not eat, although we had not eaten at all the previous day.

The girls ran to the guards and asked: 'When will our mothers come?'

The guards, Polish girls hardened by several years of imprisonment, pointed to the smoking chimney.

'There are your mothers, you little fools. Where do you think you've come to, a holiday camp? This is an extermination camp. Look at the chimney. Don't you see the flames? There your mothers are burning, your fathers will become ash, your little brothers and sisters go to heaven.'

'How cruel they are,' said my companions. 'These years of suffering have made them vengeful and sadistic. They want us to feel the pain of loss as they have. They want to torment us, who have so far escaped Nazism. They envy us who were able to live a normal life with our families while they had to suffer in camps.'

The chimney belched its black cloud of smoke with a piercing stench. It stood in the sky like an exclamation mark, confirming what the Polish girls had said.

'They're burning rubbish,' said my comrades, and stopped listening to the Polish girls. 'They won't fool us,' they said, and continued to dream of reunion. Only I wept.

Livi tried to comfort me: 'Don't cry. Mother will soon come. You'll see.'

I did not answer. I had not the heart to shatter her hopes.

We had to learn the daily routine. Reveille at dawn, followed by roll-call. We slept in our clothes, so did not need to waste time dressing.

After reveille everyone rushed to the lavatory; we had to finish there before roll-call. The lavatory was a big barracks with a raised section in the middle. Along both sides of the 'throne' were a large number of holes, so that twenty people could squat simultaneously. A long queue soon formed in front of each hole, and each girl saw to it that her predecessor did not sit for a moment longer than she absolutely needed to. Sometimes guards entered and thrashed around wildly when they thought we were sitting too long. Then we squatted two at a time, bottom to bottom, on the same hole, so that things would go quicker. Thus to sit on the hole alone was almost a luxury.

The lavatory was in an adjacent building, and we all had to be ready to urinate and defecate – under guard – at the same time. If one girl wanted to go when the rest did not, she had to wait. The worst was if one woke at night when the lavatory was shut. Then one had to use big barrels round the corner. One had to be very careful, for they were easily overturned.

Washing facilities were minimal. There was a tap where one could rinse one's hands and face after using the lavatory, but it was usually shut off. Occasionally we were allowed to shower in the bath-house, and then we were also given clean clothes. These consisted of a pair of big grey underpants, a rough vest and a dress of the same coarse grey cloth. The dresses were in only two sizes, and however we tried we never succeeded in getting ones that fitted. Some of us were swathed in big tents, while others tripped in mini-skirts, our pants, held up by string, hanging down below. We wore our own shoes, and again I pitied the girls in high heels, which soon broke. We had no stockings, but each had a man's blue handkerchief with grey edges to cover her bald head.

After using the lavatory in the morning, we had a quick rinse under the tap before we ran to roll-call. This was especially important, since we had no paper. That posed a difficult problem which taxed our inventiveness. Sometimes we might find a rough piece of cardboard from a box, sometimes we tore off a scrap from our pants or vest. Although this might be discovered when we had a change of clothes and would result in punishment, it did not deter us. We went on doing it, so that our underclothes became shorter and shorter.

Roll-call was the most important daily event in the camp. It was almost a religious rite. We were hustled out of the block three times a day. Everyone had to form up in lines of five, including the sick. Even the dying were not exempted. We were counted and re-counted, first by the *blockova*, then by an SS guard, then by another and finally by the SS commandant. The figures had to agree; I don't know what would have happened if they hadn't, for the *blockova* never risked passing on the group to the SS guard before she was sure that the number was correct. We had to stand there for hours while they counted and re-counted. If anyone felt ill or fainted, she had to lie there. No one might break the line. We had to stand to attention in wind and rain, noonday heat and freezing dawn. In our file of five, Dora always stood first and I last. Each of us hugged the girl in front of us, thus giving and receiving a little warmth.

After roll-call, breakfast was doled out. We ran quickly back, for we had to make sure that no one stole our meagre ration. We received a small piece of bread and a dab of margarine, sometimes with a teaspoonful of jam, and 'coffee', a black liquid which resembled coffee only in name. But it was hot and restored a little life to our numbed limbs. Breakfast did not take long, and the flicker of well-being was soon gone.

Then we were sitting in our bunks again, apathetically waiting for the next roll-call. The girls were still hoping to see their parents but talked less about it. As the days passed, they began, one after the other, to realize that there was no camp for the older people. Their once eager chatter ceased. Apathy overcame them too.

After the noon count, we got lunch. This consisted of a thin soup with some vegetable or other – sometimes even a scrap of meat – in it. We looked forward to it but were never satisfied. At sunset there was yet another hour-long roll-call. A mug of so-called coffee, and then we had barely time to rush to the lavatory before curfew was sounded and the light was put out for the night.

As time passed, my tears began to dry up. My body made its demands and I became hungry. Now I no longer gave away my ration: I ate everything that was given me. I began to examine my surroundings, which up to now had seemed to consist only of a chimney enveloped in grey smoke. I saw how well groomed the Polish guards were, with their long hair, neat clothes, silk stockings and smart boots. Perhaps it is possible to survive in Auschwitz, I thought, and began to ponder how they did it. I tried to talk to them but they were not sociable. They turned away as soon as I asked a question. I gave up.

One day an SS man came and handed out postcards, telling us to write home to our families. We had no families left; we knew how thoroughly the cock-feathers had cleansed the town. By this time the whole of Hungary was *Judenrein* – free of Jews. So we were suspicious and discussed it among ourselves. It had to be a trap.

'They must want to know if there are any Jews hidden somewhere. They want us to write and betray their addresses,' said Dora.

'You're right. We won't write.'

'That's best. Whoever we write to will have trouble. It isn't good to be friends with a Jew in Auschwitz.'

'But then we could get revenge on anyone who has behaved badly to us,' said Sussie.

'What about Mrs Fekete?' I said. 'She got us to give her our money and jewels and then denied they had anything.'

More and more of us remembered Hungarians who had informed on us or maltreated us, and we decided to write to them. It felt good to know that they too might now have problems. Only long after the war did I discover the purpose of these cards: to show the outside world that we were alive and well taken care of. But this did not mean that our guess had been wholly wrong.

One day someone was suddenly heard humming Beethoven's 'Für Elise'.

'What's that?' I asked. 'Who is singing?'

'Ella,' said Livi.

Ella was a girl of my age, robust and artistic. She played the piano beautifully and liked painting. Now she was walking up and down between the rows of bunks, humming. The humming became a gentle crooning, and soon she was singing at the top of her voice.

'She has gone mad,' said someone.

I went over to her and saw her burning eyes.

'What is it, Ella?' I asked.

'I'm waiting for mother. I promised to play for her. I must practise so that I'll be really good. She loves 'Für Elise'. Did you know her name's Elise? She'll be so happy. I can do it really well now. Come and listen.'

'But Ella, there is no piano here, and your mother won't be able to come.'

'Yes, mother will come. I know. Will you turn the pages for me? Come on, let's go to the piano.' And she made a sweeping gesture towards the other end of the corridor.

She turned, walked towards the 'piano' and began to sing again. Everyone looked at her in horror. What would happen? No one tried to calm her. She just went on singing. An hour later two SS men came and took her away.

'They're taking her to the gas chamber,' said the block guard, Anja.

I waited until the others had calmed down and went to the guard-room to ask Anja to tell me more. The guard-room was forbidden territory for us, and whenever one of us glanced in we were amazed at what we saw there. Platefuls of soup, masses of clothes strewn around, lipsticks, mirrors, combs and thousands of other things which we remembered had once existed in another life. How could such things be here? We could not imagine, and it was a long time before I got on good enough terms with one of the guards that I dared to ask.

But the only thing I wanted to know now was about Ella and the gas chamber. I was lucky. Anja was in a good mood and did not throw me out. What I learned from her exceeded my imagination. I now realized that the important thing was to try to get out of Auschwitz as soon as might somehow be possible. Sooner or later everyone who stayed here would end in the chimney.

There were always possibilities of getting out, for workers were needed in Germany. Anja did not know what kind of work, but she assured me that anything was better than sitting in Auschwitz, in the shadow of the crematorium. She herself hoped to get away some time, when more workers were required. When this happened, the whole block would be lined up and the SS men would choose the number they needed. Once this selection had been made, the rest would go to the gas chamber. Anja also told me that the commandant sometimes needed volunteers to work outside the camp and that these would be fetched from the various blocks in the mornings. Those girls who volunteered got an extra plate of soup as a reward. I thanked Anja for this information and left her, glad to have discovered so much.

Back in the bunk I told Dora everything I had learned. Then we went to the *blockova* to offer ourselves for work next day if they needed someone.

The following morning, when SS men came to commandeer girls to clean the guards' quarters, Dora and I managed to get accepted. Together with several others, we were led out from our barracks and, after quite a long walk, came to the gate with the big sign, '*Arbeit macht frei*' ('Work makes free'). It may be true, I thought: I was on the way to work and felt free and light of heart, despite the SS man walking behind us. Simply not having to lie idle on the bunk for a whole day meant much. And in my mind's eye I already saw the extra plate of soup I would get.

We went through the gate and into the SS quarters just outside. They gave us buckets and rags and told us to scrub the floors and the furniture. No brushes, no soap. I fetched water and began to rub the dirty planking, but, hard as I rubbed, it would not come clean. The nails hurt my hands and I asked to be allowed to go and look for some bits of brushwood. That didn't help either. The dirt remained. I was sitting in despair staring at the planks when the SS man came in. When he saw me there, he began to swear at me and at all the spoiled Jewish swine who did not want to work. It was no good explaining that it was impossible to get rid of the ingrained dirt without brushes and soap. He screamed and swore, and we had no choice but to start rubbing again.

Around noon we had a short break while the extra soup was doled out. Then there was nothing for it but to continue with our Sisyphean labour. I struggled on until the loud-speaker announced 'Feierabend', the end of the working day. The sense of freedom which the prospect of work had given me at the start of the day had long since vanished. The device on the gate seemed to smile scornfully at us as the SS man led us back into the camp.

On the road we passed some birch trees. It felt unreal to see a tree after having lived for so long in a place where nothing green existed. But perhaps it was after all not so long since we had come to Auschwitz, though it seemed to me an eternity. The birch leaves were still tender and green.

I broke off a little twig and began to stroke the heart-shaped leaves. The leaf spoke to me, comforted me and gave me hope. 'Look at me,' it seemed to say. 'I am newly born. I am free. The long winter is past. Life is beginning anew. A lovely summer is ahead.' Perhaps, perhaps, I too may dare to hope? I could not throw it away, I felt a compulsion to take it into the camp. I wanted to keep it, to show it to the others, to let its greenness speak to everyone, give hope to all. But how? I knew we would be inspected when we went in, and no one was allowed to bring in anything from outside. I was sure that not even a leaf would be allowed. I hid the tiny twig in the lining of my dress and for safety's sake hid another leaf in my mouth.

We reached the entrance to the camp. The SS guard approached to check me, touched me here and there and stroked my body. I held my breath. The twig remained undiscovered. I walked on and breathed again. I had succeeded. I could scarcely contain myself as I stood in line for roll-call and whispered to the girl closest to me that I had something exciting to show her. By the time roll-call was finished and we had returned to our bunks, the jungle telegraph had done its work, and scores of girls crowded around me to see what I had to show.

'Look, green leaves,' I said, and took out the twig.

They looked doubtfully, as though unwilling to believe their eyes. They wanted to touch the leaves.

'They're real leaves!'

'Oh, how beautiful!'

'May I hold the twig?'

'Are there really trees outside?'

'How did you get it?'

'Can I have a leaf?'

'How did you find the tree?'

'Can you get some more?'

'Let me stroke it.'

'Were there many trees?'

'What kind of trees were they?'

One question followed another, the girls hardly waiting for an answer. They took it in turns to hold the twig, touch the leaves, feel their soft touch against their cheek. When everyone had had her fill, I took one of the heart-shaped leaves and put it beneath my mattress. I wanted to press it, to keep it for as long as possible. I would take it out each evening, to remind me that there existed a life outside the camp. When I went to bed, for the first time I rejoiced at the thought of the next day. I thought of seeing the tree again and fell asleep almost happy.

Next morning I woke with the same happy feeling and hurried to roll-call, expecting to be called out. But no extra workers were needed that day.

It was not until two days later that the SS men came again and asked for two volunteers. Olga and I offered ourselves, but to my disappointment we were taken in a different direction this time.

We came to another camp. It was empty and ghostlike. No people anywhere, only empty barracks. Stiff female bodies lay scattered in front of one of the barracks, and we were ordered to pile them on a cart and pull it several hundred metres to another building. There we were to unload them and pile them on a table. Olga and I picked up the bodies, she taking the hands and I the feet. We looked at them without feeling as we lifted them. 'How young she was ...,' we commented, or, 'This one wasn't so young,' or 'She was really old.' When we had finished our work, we got our plate of soup and were taken back to our block.

The girls, waiting eagerly for more birch leaves and new tales of the green life outside, were disappointed when they saw our tired and empty faces. We had nothing to tell and wanted only to go to bed. As always, we quickly fell asleep.

Each night, as soon as we had finished our roll-call, we tried to sleep. We used to sit on the bunk in a kind of daze, less and less able to talk to one another.

One morning I woke with a curious feeling which I could not place. There were tears in my throat, but something was trying to intrude, something which felt different. Was it happiness? No, only a sad fact: 'Today is my birthday.' I was twenty, a milestone to which I had once so eagerly looked forward. But now the day brought no joy, only more tears. I remembered earlier birthdays, when I had been woken with hot chocolate in bed, flowers and presents. Instead of a birthday song I now heard the harsh cry of the SS woman: '*Raus, raus*, up with you, hurry, you swine. Out to roll-call.' I ran out, dreading a blow from her rubber club.

Livi was already up. She came over and hugged me.

'Many happy returns. Congratulations,' she said.

'Thank you. This wasn't how I'd imagined my twentieth birthday.'

'We'll have a double celebration at home when you're twenty-one to make up for it. Perhaps at last you'll get that bicycle from father. Here's a present from me.' She handed me her dearest possession, her toothbrush, which she had smuggled into the camp. 'It's yours,' she added, seeing my amazement.

I was moved. Her toothbrush. Livi was so vain about her teeth – she used to stand and brush them for hours to make them white. She had risked severe punishment to keep her toothbrush, and now she was giving it to me. I hugged her as I wept.

'Why are you crying again? Aren't you happy?'

'Of course I'm happy. I'm crying for happiness. I'm so grateful that I can be with you.'

We went towards the lavatory. Magda joined us.

'Many happy returns,' she said, and handed me a piece of brown wrapping-paper no bigger than half the palm of her hand.

'Paper?' I said. 'May I have it? Are you sure?'

I looked at the scrap of paper and wondered where she could have got hold of it. Such luxuries simply did not exist in the camp. Paper, when I was just going to the lavatory. What did it matter that it was coarse and minute? It was still paper.

'It's the best birthday present I've ever had. I shall never forget it.'

Suddenly it was fun to have a birthday. I had been remembered, after all. With presents.

That night I had diarrhoea. It was pitch dark, and I woke Dora. I did not dare to go alone to the barrel. Carefully, so as not to wake the others, we slipped down from the bunk and tiptoed to the door. It was locked and the guard was sleeping in the hut beside it. We woke her and she let us out with a sleepy oath. Outside, it was equally dark. We groped our way to the shed and I seated myself on the barrel's edge. I had colic, and it took time. Dora waited, shivering in the cold night air. We did not dare to speak. Suddenly the silence was broken by the piercing shriek of a siren. I knew that during an air-raid alarm no one was allowed outside, and realized that I must hurry back to escape punishment, but a careless movement resulted in my finding myself half buried inside the barrel. Dora burst out laughing as she helped me up.

'Do you remember the fairy tale of the girl who fell in the shit, which was later turned to gold? Tomorrow perhaps you'll be covered with gold,' she said.

I did not feel inclined to laugh. What was I to do? I had no other clothes to change into, and the night was chilly. The water tap was far away and would certainly be turned off for the night, so there was no way I could wash. We went back to the block, and the guard held her nose as we opened the door. Anja was on guard that night, one of the few who occasionally showed human feelings. I had no need to explain. She went into her hut and came back with a shirt for me to change into, and a rag to dry myself. The smell did not go when I removed my clothes, and I dared not lie down beside the others. I lay on the floor and curled up to wait for reveille.

I tried to keep count of the days, but it was not easy. Every day was like the next. One day I was surprised to find that my menstruation had begun. I went to the *blockova* to ask if she could let me have a sanitary towel. She did, at the same time comforting me with the information that this would be the last time I would have this problem. No one in the camp menstruated.

'Why is that?'

'Who knows? Perhaps because we've ceased to be women.'

'How can that be? Have they injected you?'

'No, but I think they put something in the bread – or the soup – that stops menstruation.'

'But then we'll all be sterile. And will never be able to have children.'

'Child, who wants to have children in this place? If they find anyone's pregnant, they send them straight to the crematorium.'

'But afterwards, when we're free?'

'Don't be so naïve. Do you think we'll ever be free? Do you think they'll let any of us go?'

'But the war must end some time.'

'Not for us. They'll see to it that none of us survives. They won't want to have witnesses. They'll finish us off when the war ends, if not before.'

Rosa, our *blockova*, was from Poland, and no one knew how many camps she had been in before she came to Auschwitz. She was small but shapely, with good skin, long dark hair and warm brown eyes. She was pretty, her hair fell in ringlets to her shoulders, she was always well dressed. Today she had on a grey skirt with a white woollen vest and black high-heeled shoes. I often wondered how these girls managed to dress so well, and at length I asked: 'How do you have such fine clothes? Where do you get them from?'

Rosa was in a good mood. She replied: 'It's our payment for doing their errands.'

'What do you mean?'

'We see that you behave and do everything you have to, and they give us better clothes and a bit better food.'

'Is that why Ljuba hits us?'

'She's a bit harsh, but you must forgive her.'

'The girls say she's a sadist. They think you're all evil. You tell us our parents are in the chimney, just to make us suffer.'

'You know it's true.'

'I know. But the others don't want to believe it.'

'They might as well get used to the thought. They must accept reality. One can survive only if one accepts what's happening. It doesn't help to close your eyes.'

'But Ljuba ought not to hit us with her club.'

'She's gone through a lot herself and been beaten many times. Such things make people hard. But she isn't evil.'

'You're the only person who's kind.'

'One mustn't be kind. If one is to survive, one must be hard. I may be digging my own grave.'

'No, Rosa. I promise. We'll always obey you. You must stay with us. You must go on being as you are.'

I went back to the bunk to be met by a worried Cili. She told me that she had ceased menstruating. She was puzzled because she had not slept with anyone since her last period. I calmed her by telling her what I had just learned. Several of the other girls joined in the conversation. It was a subject which concerned us all, and everyone had something to say.

'How lovely to be rid of all that misery,' said one.

'But suppose we're sterile for the rest of our lives?' I asked.

'So be it. We can't do anything about it,' said practical Dora. 'We don't know how they get this stuff into us, whatever it is.'

'We could stop drinking the coffee.'

'Or eating the soup.'

'What if it's in the bread?'

'Don't talk such rubbish. We can't give anything up. We get so little to eat, we'd never survive if we gave up anything.'

'Anyway, it's a nuisance bleeding and having pain.'

'It's funny,' said Magda. 'I always used to have headaches, but I haven't had one since we came here. Perhaps whatever they give us cures headaches too.'

'And I haven't had any stomach pains, though I was to have had my ulcer operated on before they sent us to the ghetto,' said a mother who was sufficiently young-looking not to have been sent to the left by Dr Mengele:

'I haven't had any gallstone problems,' said another.

'Perhaps they put medicine in our food too.'

'Don't be childish.'

'Why is it, then?'

'I don't know. Somehow we've all become well. Perhaps it's the change of air.'

'Do you know what I heard?' said Olga. 'They put bromide in the bread to keep us quiet. Do you think it's true?'

'Who did you hear that from?'

'Bözsi picked it up somewhere, on one of her escapades.'

Bözsi was Olga's elder sister. She was always disappearing. She was usually somewhere else when it blew for roll-call, and it was a full-time job for Olga to keep track of her. She was frightened that Bözsi would get punished, and was for ever running round to find where she was. Whenever Bözsi turned up again, she always had something to tell, an overheard conversation here, a word picked up there, so that more and more of the camp secrets became revealed to anyone who wanted to listen. But most of the girls simply rejected these stories as lies.

That was the case now. 'You're making it up,' most of the girls said, and those of us who believed her felt we could do nothing about it anyway. We simply had to accept whatever was happening. But if there was bromide in the bread, that explained a lot of things. Our passivity, so that Olga and I had been able to pile corpses into pyramids without screaming. And the way most of the girls chose not to believe their eyes or to see the flames from the chimney.

'I only hope they don't put poison in the bread one fine day. They might.'

'Let's hope they don't do that.'

One morning Ljuba was standing with the club in her hand chasing us out to roll-call. There were a thousand of us in the block, and we all had to get out at the same time. There was no way to do so quickly, for the doorway was narrow, but the guards paid no heed to this. They shouted and rained blows on us. We began to grow used to this and just tried to protect our heads. Eventually everyone was outside and forming fives, as usual. To my amazement Rosa was standing there among us, with reddened eyes, in grey prison clothes and with a blue kerchief round her head. The rest of us looked at each other. What had happened? Again it was Bözsi who knew.

Rosa had a boyfriend who was a prisoner, one of the men in striped prison clothes whom we had seen during our first night in Auschwitz. The two occasionally managed to snatch a few moments together and the previous day had been discovered by one of the SS men. Both were flogged, and what happened to the man afterwards was not known. But Rosa was dismissed from her job as *blockova*, and her beautiful hair was cut off. She was replaced by Ljuba, evil Ljuba, who so enjoyed swinging her club. We felt pity for Rosa, but even more for ourselves, when we thought of the power that Ljuba would wield now. We could only hope that Ljuba might in time suffer the same fate; we suspected that she too had a man whom she met secretly. Bözsi had more to tell us, but that had to wait until roll-call was finished.

Back in our bunks, she told of the men in the striped

clothes. Some worked on the trains as they arrived, emptying the waggons and seeing that the new prisoners obeyed the Germans' instructions. Others helped the SS men to take the selected ones to the gas chamber and then shovelled the bodies into the crematorium ovens. As a reward, they were allowed to take what they wanted from the prisoners' baggage, such as food and clothes. Many of them found jewels sewn into the clothes, and thus became the capitalists of the camp. The former were called 'Canadians' by the camp inmates, because the place where they worked flowed with milk and honey like the promised land of the East European Jews: Canada. The latter were officially called *Sonderkommando*. Because they were where everything happened, they knew too much and were potentially dangerous, so they were not allowed to live long and were replaced every three months. They had to end their lives in their workplace, the gas chamber. They knew that their days were numbered and that they had to make the best of the short time they had. They were rich, they could buy everything there was in the camp, even the girls they fancied. They took big risks when they slipped away to trysts, but since their most powerful urge, hunger for food, was satisfied, the next most powerful made its demands: hunger for love. Snatched meetings could take place behind a wall, in the lavatory or, if they were lucky, in a *blockova*'s bed.

Despite the efforts of the Germans to keep all the groups separate, it occasionally happened that we met someone who had arrived with a later transport. One day Livi ran into the block, her eyes happy.

'Hedi! Hedi! I've met Aunt Helén and Cousin Juci! I hardly recognized them without their hair.'

'Where?'

'Coming back from the lavatory. You know that block behind the lavatory? Well, they were at roll-call, and I ran towards them, although I knew the guards would beat me.

I managed to hug Aunt Helén and ask if she knew where mother was, before their *blockova* came and hit me. But it didn't hurt too much, and I'm glad I managed to hug her.'

'What did she say about mother?'

'She didn't know anything. But if she's alive, mother must be alive too. She must be in another camp. There are so many around here. Can't we go to the lavatory and try to meet her again?'

We couldn't do anything that day. And when we went there next day the block was empty. We learned that they had been taken to C camp.

Auschwitz was big – we didn't even know how big. We knew there were several camps, A, B, C etc, but not how many there were. We lived in A camp, a big area with about fifty blocks. On the other side of the barbed-wire fence we could glimpse people in B block. Above the entrance to each camp stood the device '*Arbeit macht frei*', in artificially ornate letters. I still pondered what this could mean.

A few days later, as we stood at roll-call, some SS men came, and we realized there would be a selection. They needed several hundred girls for agricultural work, and I hoped we might be among them. The five of us, Dora, Livi, Sussie, Ilu and I always stood in the same line. No one could ever part us. We thought.

The SS men began on our right, and we waited while his critical eye chose and rejected. He looked mainly at the girls' calves, and I suddenly felt as if I were in the cattle market in some Carpathian village. I half expected him to open our mouths and look into them too. He didn't, but chose girls with strong legs and broad calves. Evidently he needed oxen who could stand work in the fields. He came to our line, looked at Dora, glanced at her calves, nodded and waved her forward. The next three he dismissed with contempt. Then his eyes rested on my legs. I began to tremble and wondered if my knees would show it.

'You too,' he said, pointing at me with his riding-whip.

I took a hesitant step, thinking: 'I can't go without my sister. I can't leave her. She must come too, but how?' As the SS man moved on, I gestured to her to jump forward, but one of the guards saw it and pushed her back, hitting her several times. Soon it was all over. The man had got as many as he needed, and the others were allowed to return to the block. We, the chosen, were taken to another camp, where the bath-house was. Each of us was to have a number tattooed on the inside of her forearm, and I thought sadly of the cattle at Lăpuşel, which had names while we could not keep ours. We were to become numbers, a mass of meaningless units without identity.

I began to ponder how they had got me to regard myself as a nothing which accepted everything that was done to me, so that I even wanted to die, to satisfy their demands. How could this have happened? Was there really bromide in the bread? Or some other cause?

But this time I did not intend to meet their wishes. I knew that selection meant safety for Dora and me and death for Livi and all the others who would remain in the barracks. After every selection the remainder were taken to the crematorium. The rubbish had to be burned. Several pairs of sisters had been separated, so I went round asking if any of them would change places with Livi. They laughed at me.

'Are you mad? Don't you know what will happen to anyone who goes back?'

Yes, I knew.

Soon the now familiar routine began. We were given the evil-smelling scrap of soap, undressed and stood under the shower. After the shower we were allowed to put on clean clothes. Not the grey prison dress but civilian clothes, dresses which women had taken off on their arrival at Auschwitz and which had had a large yellow cross painted on the back, so that it could be seen from afar that we were not civilians. To my joy we were also given a vest, which I immediately used as a towel.

Before we dressed we had to have a new haircut. The stubble that had grown during the past weeks had to be shaved off. Our heads had to become billiard balls again. This time the atmosphere was more relaxed than at our first haircut, although we again stood naked before the barber. This was partly because we had begun to grow used to things and partly because my friends were happy at the prospect of leaving Auschwitz. I could not be happy; I thought only of Livi.

Now the tattooing began. The girls were told to line up in alphabetical order in front of an SS man who was sitting at a table wth a big register in front of the bath-house. Methodically he checked each girl's name and wrote a number beside it. This was tattooed on her forearm. Dora, whose surname began with A, was among the first. She showed me her forearm with the number A-7603 branded on it for eternity.

I asked: 'Are you sad?'

'I? For being tattooed? No. They're the ones who should feel sad. It's they who have behaved badly, not I.'

Dear Dora, wise as always. She reasoned that the shame always belongs to the person who has behaved badly.

'Of course I'm sad for my parents, if it's true that they have been killed, but I'm not sad about what they're doing to me. I still have my identity. They can't take that from me, however much they try. I know that I shall remain, whether they call me A-7603 or whatever.'

'You may be right. But I have a problem. Help me. I don't want to leave Livi. What shall I do?'

She did not know either. I decided to leave the queue, sit down somewhere and think of a solution. My name began with S, so I had plenty of time. I left the group, sat down as far away as I could under the fence and cried. I looked at the chimney and thought of my parents. I puzzled so intensely that I almost heard Mother's voice: 'Look after your sister.' I want to: help me, I thought in despair. I felt I had failed my mother for a second time. Had not those been her last words: 'Look after your sister'? Is this how I am looking after her? By saving myself and letting her die? No, it must not happen. If she must die, I shall die with her. Suddenly I saw the answer, which was so simple that I did not understand how I had not thought of it before. The sun stood high in the sky when, with a sense of relief, I returned to the group. Now I knew what I would do. If I could not get her out, I intended to go back to the block and be with her, share her fate whatever it might be. But how could I get there? We were watched all the time, surrounded by an electrified barbed-wire fence, guarded by SS men and their bloodhounds. No one could move without permission.

When I saw four of my former block companions arriving with cauldrons of our noonday soup, I knew what I must do. I went to them and asked if any of them would change places with me. Nina, whose sister had been selected for agricultural work, jumped at it. She did not even want my toothbrush which I offered her. We quickly hit on a plan. As soon as they had finished doling out the soup, we asked the other girls to form a ring round us, so that we could swap clothes. I took off my red flowered woollen dress and put on the grey prison clothes which Nina had taken off. She put my dress on and went to look for her sister. I took the empty cauldron and went off with the three others through the camp gate, where the sentence *'Arbeit macht frei'* grinned once more at me. The cauldron was heavy, but I felt good. I knew I had chosen right.

Inside the block the atmosphere was grim. It was always dark in there, but today the darkness seemed even deeper. It was deathly silent. Only a few snivels could be heard. Bözsi was the first to notice me. She looked at me as though she had seen a ghost.

'Hedi, what are you doing here?'

'I've come back. Where's Livi?'

'Are you crazy? Do you know what they're going to do to us?'

'Of course I know. But I don't want to be saved without my sister.'

'You must be mad. Your sister? We've all got to think of ourselves. I've a sister too, but if I'd been selected I wouldn't have bothered if my sister had been left behind.'

'Where is Livi?' I asked again.

'She must be in the lavatory. I'll go and fetch her,' she muttered irritably.

But now Livi came running back. Someone had already told her. Weeping, she threw herself round my neck.

'Hedi, Hedi, you're back! Thank God!'

We both cried as we hugged each other, thinking: it doesn't matter what happens as long as we can be together.

Life went on in this antechamber of death. Night came, and we were two fewer in the bunk. Dora and another of the girls were gone. We missed Dora but were happy that we could turn over without waking all the others. Morning brought the usual routine of waking, the rush to the lavatory and roll-call. Magda took Dora's place at the head of our file. Magda was another of my friends and former classmates, a little pale girl with burning black eyes and a quick intelligence.

As we waited to be counted, we thought that the SS commandant would soon come and send us to the gas chamber. But nothing happened. Not that day or the next.

After roll-call we were sent back to the block and sat down again on the bunk like frightened sparrows to wait for the end. The days dragged on. Having nothing to do meant that we all had the same thought, and we felt relieved each evening that we had been allowed to live another day. To what purpose? Did it mean anything that we lived? Would it not have been better if we had been allowed to die quickly, so that we could have been spared the pain of grieving for our lost loved ones, and this unending anxiety about the future? But we wanted to live.

We went on waiting for death. A few days later, to my surprise, we were sent out to work, to another camp where new barracks had been built, to get rid of the rubbish, pile the remaining boards into heaps and tidy everything up. It was a relief to work after the weeks of idleness. We had not done much before the whistle went to summon us to roll-call. My heart was in my mouth. Now, I thought, now the hour has come. Now we shall go to the gas chamber. There can be no other explanation for calling roll-call at such an unusual time. We formed into line and awaited our fate. The *kapo* – work leader – simply announced that the work group from Block 35, our block, was to return immediately. We grasped each other's sweating hands and marched away to, we assumed, death.

Back in our camp, I saw two SS men approach the block. They went to the *blockova* and I tiptoed to her window. I tried to listen. I wanted to know what was going to happen. I heard them ask Ljuba if all the girls in her block had undergone work-selection. When they learned that a hundred or so had not gone through the process, they ordered us to form up and announced that they needed more workers.

When the block guard blew his whistle for us to form up, with the unprocessed hundred at the front, I ran back to calm my friends and tell them what I had heard. I had a plan. I tried to get in with my file of five among the first hundred, but did not succeed. They knew each other and were well aware that if any outsiders got among them it would mean that some of them might not be chosen. So I decided that we should line up as the first five after the hundred.

I looked at my 'children' and was not happy with what I saw. They were four spindly girls, emaciated and wretched, no good for work. Magda, the smallest, and the other three, who were a little taller, stood there pale, with shrunk cheeks. I realized something had to be done. I took out the little piece of bread I had left and stuffed it into Livi's cheeks so that she would look a little sturdier. I slapped her cheeks several times to make them rosier and healthier-looking, and told her to hold herself up to give an impression of strength and determination. I did the same to the other three. Now there was nothing to do but wait and hope. The SS man walked slowly past the lines of the hundred and picked out a few here, a few there. For once he did not look at their legs but at the general impression each made. I grew more and more nervous the closer he approached, crossed my fingers and offered a silent prayer.

Now he had reached the last file of the hundred, and I held my breath as he chose two and turned his eyes to my file. It had worked: he had not noticed that he had come to the end of the hundred. He pointed at Livi, Sussie, Magda and me. I breathed again. Saved. I led my 'chickens' to join the others who had been chosen, but felt a stab in my breast when I looked at Ilu, left alone staring apathetically at nothing. It was the last time I saw her.

When the selection had been completed, we were taken to the bath-house to be disinfected and reclothed. We were given civilian dress with a yellow cross on the back, and Dutch clogs for those whose shoes were in shreds. Olga, who was given a pair of these, complained that they were too hard. Like the rest of us, she had never seen clogs before and had to learn how to walk in them. When we were lined up before the man with the register, I assumed that the previous procedure would be repeated, but instead of the tattooer's needle I saw a pile of numbered badges on strings, which we had to put round our necks.

All this took a couple of hours. Then we were marched to the station, where a train was waiting. We sat on the wooden seats and chattered eagerly, wondering where we were going. But these questions were left unanswered. The SS guards threatened to beat us unless we shut up. We tried to restrain our excitement and fell quiet. I waited impatiently for the train to leave. As long as we stayed here, anything might happen. The minutes crawled slowly. I did my best to will the train into motion, but nothing happened.

I do not know how long we had been waiting when, as though in a mist, I heard my surname called. I went to the window and saw a girl running from carriage to carriage asking if there was anyone of that name. When I replied, she told me she had been working in the kitchen and that a man from the bakery had begged her to see if any of his family was on the train. Surely it could only have been my father? Livi and I questioned her, but although she could not give us much information, we were convinced it was he. We were elated, but at the same time sad that we were leaving just as we had succeeded in tracing him. Then our joy that he was alive won, and when, a moment later, the train started, we wanted to sing. We had left the death camp. Father was alive. What did it matter that we had no idea where we were going? From now on things must surely improve. When one has sunk to the nadir of hopelessness, a change can only be for the better.

The girls sang old Hungarian songs, and I joined in. My voice felt rusty and untuned, and it took a while before I found it, but soon I was belting out one sugary melody after another.

4   Hamburg

Our exhilaration faded as the monotonous thumping of the train made us drowsy. We stopped singing. One after the other fell asleep. I wondered: how long had we been at Auschwitz? It felt like a lifetime, but when I looked at the landscape through the train window I realized it could not have been more than a few months. We had arrived at Auschwitz on the night of 17 May – 27 Ijar according to the Jewish calendar, a date I would never forget. On that day I would say Kadish, the prayer for dead parents, as long as I lived.

The train passed through deep green country. It was beautiful after the desolation of Auschwitz. What was it? Meadows or pasture? I don't remember, but it must have been grass, for crops would have looked paler. Everything was so peaceful, one could not imagine that a war was raging around us. For a moment I thought perhaps it had all been a nightmare, that I was on my way to Aunt Regina at her farm. But a glance at my companions assured me that the nightmare was reality. Their sleeping faces were relaxed, but they all bore signs of the months that had passed. Emaciated bodies, incipient wrinkles, bald skulls. Only reality can create such images.

A fly walked along the window frame, and I wondered if it too felt a sense of liberation at having escaped from Auschwitz? I supposed not. The fly had not been a prisoner; it was free to fly away when and where it wished. And now it chose to go with us, to see where we were being taken. Unlike the dog which had watched us in the park as we left Sighet, the fly could accompany us all the way. I looked tenderly at the fly: a living thing that cared, or so I could fantasize.

How long did the train journey take? I don't remember that either. Only that when I woke we were at a big station, Hamburg. Many trains were crowded there. Ours went on past the station to the port, where it stopped in front of huge warehouses. A board said 'Wilhelmshafen'. So this was our destination. Here our new life would start, beyond the shadow of the chimney.

The sun shone and the water glittered as we were ordered to leave the train and go to the warehouse which was now to be our home. We climbed the steps and entered a big hall with gigantic windows overlooking the River Elbe. Beds were laid out in two tiers, and we ran to claim one. Livi and I had just seated ourselves in the upper tier by the window, for the view, when an SS man shouted that no one was allowed to share. So Livi moved to the bed below, and I stretched out, happy to feel again how it was to be alone in one's own bed, to lie on one's back with arms outstretched, to twist and turn without being shouted at to keep still.

The last rays of the afternoon sun illuminated the warehouse. The reflections of the waves trembled on the walls. The bright hall was a gaudy contrast to our dark barrack room. We had come from hell to heaven. They gave us bread and coffee which tasted of coffee. Then I fell asleep and dreamed that I was playing with goldfish which chased each other untroubled by the pike lurking behind a rock.

I was woken by a whistle and a summons to roll-call. Our first morning in our new prison gave us hope, although the new routine was not very different from the old. We had to learn to make our beds, tucking in the blanket in a special way so that the mattress would be as flat as a tabletop. Then we experienced an almost forgotten luxury, washing ourselves in basins that stood at one end of the warehouse. We lined up for roll-call and were divided into small groups. The files of five were formed into groups of thirty who were taken to the harbour. There we were put into a boat which hooted and set off up the Elbe. Had it not been for the ruins along the bank, we might have supposed ourselves on a summer holiday. None of us had ever travelled by boat before. The salt water splashed our clothes, and the wind brushed our cheeks as we stood at the rail holding each other's hands.

In half an hour we arrived at our destination, Schindler's Wharf. We landed and were lined up under a tree for the commandant to choose a *kapo* – a leader. He looked closely at the thirty smallish girls, and his eyes rested on me. He looked me up and down, down and up.

'Can you speak German?'

I thought of Rose, the little Dutch girl I had met in Auschwitz, and the trouble she had taken to teach me German. I said boldly, 'Yes.'

'Then you must be *kapo* and see that everyone works hard. I don't want to hear any complaints. Work well and you'll be well treated. Anyone who doesn't work will have no food. Understood?'

I felt both sad and happy. I didn't want to be a policewoman, but my appointment would bring advantages. The *kapo* always got the first ladleful of soup, which meant a good helping of vegetables, sometimes even meat.

I was so engrossed in my thoughts that I scarcely heard the work leader assigning our various tasks. We had to clear bomb-damage, dig ditches, carry sacks of cement and form a long chain to pass bricks. Whole bricks went into one pile, broken ones in another. I jumped to attention as the guard, a middle-aged soldier, addressed me. He looked nice, and asked my name. He wanted to know how old I was, where I came from and how I had come to be here. It was the first time for months that anyone had spoken to me as a human being. It transpired that this soldier, Hermann, had daughters of my age, and he was much upset when he heard what I had to tell him. He tried to comfort me, assuring me that things would be better now that we were allowed to work.

So it turned out. Hermann was kindly and urged me not to make the girls work too hard. I told them to pretend to put their backs into it and make sure they weren't caught. We appointed one of us to keep watch and leaned chatting on our spades around the ditch that had to be dug. When she saw anyone approaching, she called the password, 'Eighteen', and we started digging. I went round exhorting them: 'Dig harder! *Arbeiten! Schnell, schnell!'* – adding softly in Hungarian: 'Don't overdo it.' The SS man moved off, and we returned to doing nothing, while Hermann turned a blind eye.

We had scarcely noticed that the sun was high in the sky when the whistle went for lunch. We were led into big, bright rooms where other workers, prisoners of war from the Baltic States and France, were already seated around laid tables. We stared in disbelief at the white tableclothes, china plates, spoons, glasses and carafes of clear water. In the centre of the table stood a large basket of sliced dark bread. We continued to stare, fearing it might rise and vanish before we had got our teeth into it. As soon as we sat down, a girl in a white coat came in with a cauldron of steaming soup. She served us. It was thick and contained vegetables, meat and macaroni. When I cautiously stretched a hand towards the bread, Hermann told us to eat as much as we wanted, and when it was finished a fresh basket was brought. We drank the soup slowly, to prolong the pleasure, but when our plates were empty we were asked if we would like more. We ate and ate, until even we were full.

Next morning we still hardly dared to believe it had been true, and looked forward to another such lunch. It had been the first time for many weeks that we had been able to go to bed without being racked by hunger. Life became tolerable. But not for long.

A few days later the camp commandant announced that we were not entitled to the privileges which Schindler's workforce enjoyed. We were not prisoners of war, we were not even Balts, we were Jews. The boat trips to the yard stopped. Hermann was moved elsewhere and we were taken by a disagreeable SS man several kilometres on foot to a bomb-site. There we were allotted our tasks; they were the same as before, but our treatment was very different. When the lunch break came, we queued up in front of a cauldron, and the guard doled out soup – not the wonderful thick soup we had had at Schindler's but something close to the watery pigswill at Auschwitz. But at least it was hot, and we sat on the ground with our tin bowls and dreamed of being back at Schindler's.

In the evenings after work we washed, ate our meagre supper and enjoyed the brief hour we had before sleep. It stayed light late, and we used those minutes for washing our clothes, resting and dreaming. As I lay on my bunk, I could talk to the river which rolled heavy and dark outside the window. It greeted me from the forests of Czechoslovakia where it had its source, not far from my childhood home. I felt that it and I were old friends. I found new friends too. On the floor above were some Italian prisoners of war, who tried to talk to us through the window. When they discovered who we were, they found a way to send us presents. They tied parcels to the end of a rope and let it hang from their window till it reached ours. We untied the parcel and sent a letter back on the rope. They gave us cigarettes, chocolate and jam, all of which we appreciated not merely for their own sake but as a sign that someone was interested in us.

So we were comparatively well off at Wilhelmshafen, and wanted to thank our new friends who were responsible for this. Few of us spoke any foreign language, so that I became important to all those girls who wanted to write letters of thanks. I was happy to be the general correspondent, and looked forward as much as they to the 'answer to the answer', which always meant a new parcel.

There were also Soviet prisoners of war in the warehouse. They looked at us with interest but never contacted us as the Italian and, later, the French prisoners did. This may have been because of the language problem – none of us knew Russian – or because they had less to spare. One day we learned that Stalin's son was among them, which gave rise to fantasies that one night the Soviets would come to free him, and release us too. That Stalin did not care about his son we did not know, nor that any 'liberation' by the Soviets would merely have meant another imprisonment.

Simultaneously with our arrival in Hamburg, a group of women had come from Theresienstadt, the family camp in Czechoslovakia. They were mostly Czech but included some Germans. Their history of suffering was much longer than ours, for they had been interned at the outbreak of war. But they had been allowed to keep their hair, for which we envied them. One of them, Ursula, had been born in Hamburg. She had left to marry a Czech and had a little son whom she often talked about. She hoped that he and her husband were still safe in Theresienstadt. We asked her to tell us about Hamburg. We knew only the warehouse and a short stretch of the Elbe, but she brought to our eyes the city's broad avenues and handsome buildings, the Old Town and the Church of St Nicholas, the parks and museums, many of which were now in ruins.

Ursula considered trying to escape. She told us which road she would take and where she would go, but always ended by wondering if anyone would dare to hide her. She felt too unsure of her former friends to try to carry out her plan. Anyway she did not dare while I was in Wilhelmshafen. I hope she later found the courage and succeeded.

Our group from Hungary and some girls from Czechoslovakia were moved to the suburb of Altona. Our new camp consisted of five wooden barracks surrounded by a barbed-wire fence. This was much worse than the warehouse: we would miss the parcels, and our view over the Elbe. Now we no longer lived under the same roof. Each barrack had its *blockova*, chosen from among us by the commandant, and we were also overseen by women SS guards, *Aufseherinnen*, indoors, and by SS men outside. The commandant was a tall, blond SS *Unterscharenführer*, or group leader, whom we called Schara. We tried to make ourselves scarce when he appeared, for he was liable to strike out for no reason. Elegant, like all SS men, in his immaculate uniform and shining boots, he stalked the yard with icy staring eyes, ever on the hunt for a victim.

I quickly became one. A girl named Cili told him how I had encouraged the girls to idle at work. My first evening in the new camp, he came up to me and struck me twice savagely across the face. Before I could think of a reason, he said, 'You are no longer a *kapo*. Tomorrow you will report to your new *kapo* for orders.' This turned out to be Cili.

I was not particularly sorry. I was not suited to be a *kapo*.

The Italians who had sent us parcels in Wilhelmshafen left, and French prisoners of war took their place. The Frenchmen were much richer – or more generous? The parcels became bigger and more frequent. Most of us acquired a 'parcel friend'. They were strictly forbidden to communicate with us; if they were found out, they would be shot. But this did not frighten them. They continued to find opportunities of passing small packets to us, and words of encouragement. It is hard to say which meant the more to us, the parcels or the words.

Our schooling had taught us to love everything French – France, the French language, French poets, French novelists, French people. And now here were these kind Frenchmen, talking French and giving us presents. One look at them, and we were all infatuated. One girl after another came to me to tell me that she was in love and to ask me to help write a love-letter.

I too fell in love.

My group was ordered to a new place of work, a building-site. Small houses were being built for those who had been bombed out, and we had to help with every kind of work. The hardest, but the most sought-after, was carrying the fifty-kilo sacks of cement from the camp to the foundations. This had the advantage that one was able to walk a hundred metres on one's own.

Olga and I were carrying one of the sacks the first time I met Paul.

It was not his face that attracted me, and certainly no sense of inward beauty. Of that I knew nothing. It was just that as he passed he dropped, as though by chance, a packet at my feet, the way a medieval lady might have dropped her handkerchief. Not until the next day, when the same thing happened, did my feelings emerge. I wrote a letter of thanks, and next time we passed I slipped it to him. We even exchanged a few words.

'What is your name?'

'Edwige. What's yours?'

'Paul.'

With that he was gone. Paul was not especially good-looking. He was of average height, with dark hair and dark eyes. But he spoke French. My heart raced, and suddenly everything became easier to bear. The sun was shining, the sacks were lighter, the surroundings more friendly. I did what I had to mechanically, living only for the moment when our eyes could meet. In the evenings I wrote letters and wove dreams.

So the days passed and summer became autumn. It began to rain and was darker now when we lined up for roll-call. We had to march to our work in hail and sleet, still in our thin summer clothes. At the end of the day it felt good to go back indoors. Although the barrack was unwarmed, it was protected from the wind, and we could huddle under our blankets. The novelty of having French comrades had faded, and we felt very low. The worst thing was the hunger.

To give us something else to think about, we formed study groups. Every girl had to write down poems she remembered, and in the evenings we read them aloud. Hungarian and Romanian poets, and of course the French poets whom we loved best: Baudelaire, Villon, Verlaine, Géraldy. But where could we find pencils and paper? We cajoled the odd kindly guard and the French prisoners, searched rubbish heaps and eventually managed to amass a few writing-materials. After a few days we were seated in a circle writing, and a few days later held our first reading. We invited guests from the other blocks and declaimed grandly. We repeated this, evening after evening, and in time ventured our own little poems and stories. Our feelings began to flower. Hidden talents peeped forth: one girl could draw, another act. We entertained each other and for a while forgot our hunger.

Best of all was when Grete imitated us. She was a bullying *blockova* in her forties, whom we feared and hated, but she turned out to be a considerable actress. There was never any doubt whom she was imitating. When she went to the mirror and pretended to elbow aside someone who was standing there, it was our vain Giza to the life. Only then did we realize how obediently we made way as soon as Giza indicated that she wanted to look at herself.

When we had laughed ourselves tired, Grete went to the mirror again, studied herself and grimaced. Now it was me they were laughing at, for each morning I stuck out my tongue at my own reflection. I decided at once to stop doing this, though I still thought I looked like a monkey. My hair had begun to grow again and stuck up like hedgehog quills, my face was grey, my skin peeling, and my clothes were several sizes too large. I did not like what I saw in the piece of mirror, and envied those girls who still had their hair or who managed to look beautiful even without hair and in rags.

Then Grete squatted in a corner, hunched her back and drooped her head between her shoulders like a winged crow. Her stockings hung down like sausages, her face was scared and furtive. This was Ladi, who made a habit of hiding in corners to avoid the heaviest cement sacks.

The romance with Paul continued – or anyway, the parcels continued to come. I thought he was in love with me. How could I know that these parcels and warm feelings only betokened pity? We were skeletal and forlorn in our rags; they had their own clothes, better treatment, better food, Red Cross parcels every month and other privileges.

We saw each other daily, exchanged stolen words and wrote to each other. I mobilized my best French and penned the prettiest love-letters I could. When I thought of him in the evenings, my heart was filled with something I had not felt for a long while. Puppy love? Happiness? I did not care that I risked severe punishment.

I was woken at dawn by the shrill sound of a whistle. My first action was to feel under the mattress. Was the bread there? I had saved a crust the previous evening, and it might have been stolen. No, there it was. Good not to have to feel completely empty. I ate it before I had properly opened my eyes. As I did so, I heard shouts and the sound of blows approaching: the SS woman, fat Marie.

'Out, out! How long are you going to lie there idling? Up and make your beds! Up at once! Out to roll-call!'

Best to get up before she reaches my bed with her rubber club. I jumped down from the top bunk, made my bed quickly and made sure that my paper with the poems was well hidden beneath the mattress. I ran out to the wash-house for a quick hand-rinse, then back to drink a little of the thin brownish liquid which was being doled out. At least it was hot. After a few swallows I was out at roll-call. As at Auschwitz, we were counted when we woke, counted when we went to work, counted when we returned and counted before we went to bed. We must have been precious to them, they counted us so often.

It was still dark outside, and we had to stand and wait for the camp commandant. But that day the waiting did not seem long. I thought only that I would soon see Paul. He had written in his last letter that he would meet me in the empty hut at our work-place, where we could find privacy to talk. I wondered how we could do this without being discovered, but I was determined to try, despite the danger. Suddenly I was recalled to reality. Olga, who was standing in front of me, fell flat on the ground. She had low blood pressure and had difficulty in standing motionless for a long time. I tried to help her up but she had fainted, so I asked to be allowed to fetch a little water.

After a few moments she regained consciousness. We waited on. It was daylight by the time the commandant arrived, counted us and gave the signal for our departure. The camp gate was opened and we marched off to our work in rain and a gusting wind. I was freezing in my thin summer dress, and my shoes sloshed through the puddles, but it didn't matter. I was going to meet Paul.

I had just deposited my tenth sack of cement when he appeared. As he passed me, he whispered, 'Now.' I glanced round and, since the guard was a good way off and no German was in sight, slipped off to meet him. Inside the hut we fell into each other's arms. He whispered my name in French: 'Edwige.' I waited for more words of love, but Paul was no romantic teenager. He was a man in the prime of life, who needed a woman. Suddenly I encountered something different from what I had expected.

'Edwige, *tu sais* – you're not a child any longer, I'd like to – you know – with you …'

His right hand groped under my dress while his left fingered my breast. I felt as though he had struck me. I looked at him and was frightened. His eyes were aflame. What did he want? I freed myself and ran out. My heart was beating with fear, not love. Of course I knew what he wanted. But one didn't do such things – *I* didn't.

A little later, as I returned with a sack of cement, the SS commandant came on a routine check, which included a visit to the hut. My old-fashioned upbringing had saved us both.

Back in the camp, I discovered that my poems had gone. While we were at work, the SS had searched the beds. Magda's beloved Dostoevsky, Teresa's crumbs of bread, Olga's pencil – everyone had lost something. Complaints and oaths were to be heard from every bed. We were saddest at losing our poems, stories and writing-materials. Now our literary efforts would have to begin anew.

But we had no time to grieve. We had to build a fire under the big wash-pot so that we could bathe before the lights were put out. Ten of us had to use the same water, and it was important that the girls who had best succeeded in the art of keeping free from vermin should bathe first. Bugs and lice were common guests with us, and most of us had scabies. Five were still 'clean', so we drew lots, as did the five who were to follow.

The fire beneath the pot spread a pleasant glow, and we enjoyed watching the flickering flames and thinking of the bath to come. The fire awoke many memories, and we began to exchange them.

'Do you remember when they cooked plum jam in the garden at home? They kept the fire going all night under the great pots, and someone had to keep stirring till it became a black, soggy mass. Sometimes it took several days and nights. We children were allowed to stay and listen to the grown-ups' stories.'

'When we get home, we'll have stories to tell.'

'*If* we get home.'

'Don't be silly. Whom will you tell the stories to? Who'll want to listen? Our families are all here. There'll be no one who hasn't been through all this.'

'You're right.'

'The water's hot now. Who's first tonight?'

I was the lucky one. I undressed quickly and stepped into the pot. The hot water felt wonderful, but I could not enjoy it for long – the others made sure that I washed quickly. I was the fortunate possessor of a stub of soap and rubbed myself happily.

'If you lend me your soap, you can borrow my toothbrush,' said Olga. A fair exchange.

When I climbed out of the bath, I had to put on my old dirty clothes. I shook them to freshen them a little and went back to the barracks, where the evening soup was being given out. I didn't want to stay while the others bathed and the water gradually became greyer. After the soup we talked for a while about our vanished poems, and of the chances of re-creating them. When the lights went out, we went with them.

Next day I tried to avoid Paul. I thought he must be angry with me, and I did not want to hear it. I changed work with Bözsi. She took my cement sacks, and I took her place in the brick chain. When the whistle went for lunch, Böszi gave me a packet. It was from Paul. My heart beat faster: at least he wasn't angry. The packet contained a piece of bread, two cigarettes, an apple, a handkerchief and a letter. I shared the bread and the apple with Livi, hid the handkerchief and the cigarettes and, as I began to eat, read the letter. Paul did not refer to what had happened the previous day. He wrote that he had heard on the English wireless that the Germans had suffered defeats on every front and that the war could not last much longer. He knew what it meant for us to hear news. Such tidings were like vitamin-injections; they helped us to endure. I told the others, and that evening we felt much less hungry.

Two days later my handkerchief was stolen. When I felt under the mattress, my fingers touched only its rough surface. My beautiful soft cotton handkerchief, my beloved sole possession, was gone. I began to cry. Livi heard me from the bottom bunk.

'What's happened? Are you ill?'

'My handkerchief's gone.'

'Perhaps it's slipped further in.'

'No, it's been stolen.'

'Well, it's nothing to cry about.'

'I got it from Paul. He likes me. He isn't angry with me. I felt his hand caressing me every time I touched it.'

'Don't be stupid. You've lost many more important things. Are you going to cry for a handkerchief?'

I couldn't help it. It felt as though I had lost Paul. I cried, and swore at the evil thief who had stolen it. It was not a guard or the *blockova* this time, I knew, otherwise much else would have gone.

Our bullying *blockova* Grete was sacked. She had become overbold and cheeked the SS guards once too often. One day when we returned from work we found that Teri had been appointed *blockova*. I was happy. Teri was from Sighet, she belonged to our group, so now we might hope for favours. Since Grete had never liked me, my friends and I had always got the thinnest soup and never any extra when there was some left over. When we queued, everyone tried to be first so as to get the most vegetables. But all depended on the *blockova* who ladled it out. Everyone watched the ladle. If it descended only an inch or two, we knew only thin liquid would come; if it dug deep, there might be turnips, beetroots, perhaps potatoes, onions, even, if one was lucky, meat. The *kapo* and *blockova* used these occasions to favour their friends and those who ran their errands. Soup was their currency.

Teri was very fair and never tried to buy favours. But her sense of justice demanded that her friends should enjoy the superior soup to which she as *blockova* was entitled. Whenever she saw any of her friends, she dug the ladle deep. This worked well for a few evenings, but soon the others began to protest. So Teri promised not to look at who was in the queue; she let someone else hold the plates and ladled mechanically, without lifting her eyes from the pot. That evening my stomach rumbled discontentedly. Later we debated the situation and decided we must give her some signal when we approached. Whoever was handling the plates would cough, and that would signify to Teri that the next ladleful would be for a friend. This worked for a few evenings, but soon the others spotted our ruse. In the end we had to accept the inevitable and take our chance.

Teri was sorry but did not want to be accused of unfairness.

It was the evening before Yom Kippur, the Day of Atonement. Livi was feeling ill. She was pale and thin, more tired than usual, and for some days had been finding it difficult to work. After our evening soup we decided to take her to the sick bay. This was in one of the barracks and held five or six beds. There was a nurse there, but no doctor. Nor was one needed; we were not meant to be ill.

Hanka, the nurse, looked at Livi's eyes. 'You've got jaundice. You should eat a lot of sweet things,' she added ironically.

'That might be arranged,' I said, pretending to ignore the sarcasm. 'Paul will help us.'

'Can I stay here for a few days?' asked Livi. Not to have to stand at roll-call, not to march to work, not to carry bricks – to rest.

The idea made me uneasy and I tried to dissuade her. I remembered the risks that illness had carried at Auschwitz. Besides, we had just learned that we were to be moved again to another camp. So we decided to wait.

On our way back to the block we saw that the religious among us had begun to gather for prayer. The pale autumn sun was setting. It was time for Kol Nidre, the prayer that precedes the Day of Atonement, and the rumour had spread that someone had a prayer book. They were determined to fast, despite all efforts to dissuade them. I had difficulty in understanding their blind faith when I saw them the next morning, working as usual without having touched food. They would not even swallow water, and by the end of the day they could scarcely stand. They staggered back to camp, their minds doubtless on the evening soup. But instead of the soup, a surprise awaited us. We were to move that evening. We must wait for the lorries, and no soup would be doled out until we had been installed in our new camp. Was it deliberate that our move had been arranged to take place on this day? We didn't know, but we were convinced that they had decided to make us wait for our soup.

After an hour or so the lorries arrived and took us to another suburb, Eidelstedt. The barracks there were identical to those at Altona. We learned that the camp belonged to a building firm which had hired us to help erect dwellings for the people who had been bombed out of Hamburg. Now at last we received our soup. We ate it, and the enfeebled fasting women were able to rest.

Next morning fat Marie, the worst of the SS women, was soon among us, her eyes betraying her pleasure at the portunity to hit anyone who was slow to move. I could never understand how a girl of my age could be so evil. For some reason I had expected better treatment from the women guards than from the men, but with one exception the reverse was the case. Blonde, dreamy Edith did not seem to enjoy beating. She went round with her club as the others did, and sometimes shouted at us, but she seldom struck us.

When our tasks were allotted, the foreman detailed me to look after his hut. I was to be his personal servant, cleaning it and keeping it tidy, and seeing that a good fire was burning when he came during his break. I was delighted; I thought I might be able to hide Livi there when she felt more than usually bad.

The foreman turned out to be taciturn but kind. When I asked if I might bring my sister there, he nodded almost imperceptibly and murmured that I should make sure no SS guard discovered her. I fetched Livi and made her lie down in a corner while I cleaned the floor.

Our move meant that we lost contact with our Frenchmen. Doubtless it was part of the SS's plan to break us. They kept moving us around to prevent our dropping roots anywhere and establishing some attachment that might lend us strength. They wanted to underline their power and our helplessness.

But there were French prisoners of war working here too, and they were as considerate to us as their compatriots at Altona. New Frenchmen gave us new parcels. I learned that they lived in the same quarters as Paul, and one of them promised to take a letter to him. I wrote telling him of Livi's illness, and next day I received a packet from him. The traffic began again. He sent various sweet things for her, and the other girls helped by giving their rations of jam, or the chocolate they received in parcels, in exchange for whatever we could give them. I thought of asking the foreman if he could help, but when I saw his lunch, which consisted of a soup made from apple peelings, I realized he had little to spare, and certainly nothing in the way of sweet things. But the sweets and rest which Livi did get had their effect. She improved each day and soon was able to work again.

One day the foreman told me that I was to help him fetch boards from a timber-yard. I assumed that an SS guard would accompany us, for none of us was ever allowed out without being overseen. When just the two of us got into the car, I was surprised but did not like to ask. He looked round before pressing the starter, muttering something about 'damned guards'; he was evidently not prepared to wait. When we reached the timber-yard, I was ordered to wait while the foreman went into the office. I sat on a pile of boards, amazed to find myself for once alone. It struck me that this might be an opportunity to escape. But where to? I did not know the city, or any of its inhabitants. And with the yellow cross on my back, how far would I get before the SS recaptured me?

My thoughts were interrupted by a German worker who asked what I was doing there. I told him I was waiting for my foreman, but he wanted to know more. I explained how we had been dragged from our homes, how my parents had been murdered in Auschwitz and how we were now performing slave labour. When I had finished, he left without a word. I could not understand why, but soon he returned with a friend and asked me to repeat what I had just said. When I did, they looked at each other, said loudly: 'The swine!', and walked off. I guessed that they must have been Socialists – real Socialists, not National Socialists (Nazis) – who were opposed to Hitler and his policies. But if such people existed, why did they do nothing? Why did they not protest? Why did they let it all happen?

The foreman returned. We loaded the boards into the car and drove back to the building-site. That evening I told the other girls about my trip, and the questions I had asked myself. None of them knew the answer.

We became accustomed to our new camp and our new work. To encourage us to work harder, the building firm announced that they would reward us with coupons. They wanted to give us the chance to earn more if we worked harder; these coupons would be currency in a canteen which was being opened in one of the barracks. There one could buy sauerkraut, herring, mussels, sometimes even jam and small bits of evil-smelling Limburger cheese. This resulted in a welcome addition to our diet and a welcome break in our monotonous routine. The sauerkraut was especially appreciated. But unfortunately the reward system did not last long. At first all these delicacies were available, then gradually their number shrank, and before long the canteen was closed. And I was moved from my cosy hut. Now I had to stand in the brick chain with the rest and freeze in my thin dress.

It became colder and colder. One day a lorry arrived with warmer clothes. Civilian coats and jumpers, which other women had surrendered on their arrival at

Auschwitz, were doled out to us for the winter. I was lucky enough to get a long blue coat, unlined admittedly but still a coat. Most of the girls just got jumpers. That these clothes were now adorned with big yellow crosses did not bother us. Star of David or cross on our backs, what did it matter?

One of my toenails became infected. How it happened I don't know, but my toe swelled, and soon I could not put my shoe on. I bandaged my foot with rags and limped on one shoe. Eventually the guard got tired of seeing this and sent me to the sick bay. The 'doctor' examined my foot and produced an ointment. It was the same ointment she used for all ailments – there was nothing else: an evil-smelling thing called Ichtiol, which she rubbed on wounds and inside your throat. Now I got some on my toe. I don't know if it helped, but at least it didn't hurt. My toe healed slowly, as did all ailments, thanks to under-nourishment and lack of medicines. I had to limp on my bandaged foot for several months.

Hamburg was bombed several times a week. We became used to the alarms and always greeted them with joy. Those were my happiest moments. The SS guards ran to the shelter, some of the girls hid under the table with blankets over their heads, but I stood at the window, looking at the sky and rejoicing at each new explosion. However close the bombs fell, I was never afraid. I thought only of the sight that would greet us in the morning: streets in chaos, ruined houses, our work-place pitted with craters. Living daily as a neighbour of death anaesthetizes fear of it; it becomes a friend.

Vera was afraid; she was one of those who hid when the alarm sounded. Her suffering had begun long before I heard of Hitler's 'Final Solution'. When the Germans occupied Czechoslovakia, she was interned in Theresienstadt, that model camp in which the inmates were allowed to live almost normal lives. They kept their clothes and their hair; families stayed together. Vera was then a teenager and in love with a young man whom she eventually married. Soon after their wedding they were parted, and Vera was transported to Hamburg. When I met her, I was impressed by her exalted calm, stoical smile and lovely blonde hair. Her almond-shaped eyes radiated warmth and repose. I was always surprised when I looked at her: she seemed self-sufficient, unaffected by what happened round her, an island, untouchable, invulnerable. She did her work with a small, quiet smile, and no one ever heard her complain.

Gradually she seemed to be growing a little plumper. I did not understand how this could be, with our starvation rations. Then one day she told me she was pregnant. For nine months she had managed to conceal it, but now the baby was almost due. What would happen? In our camp there was room only for women who could work. Anyone pregnant would be returned to Auschwitz.

'What will happen?' I asked.

'I shall manage. I shall bear the child when my time comes.'

'But what then? How will you look after it? Do you think you'll be able to go on working?'

'I hope so. I can hang the baby on my back, the way peasant women do in China. They go back to the fields at once.'

'I'm afraid that won't be easy.'

'I'm not afraid of anything. I intend to fight for my child.'

'I'd better tell Teri. She may be able to talk to Schara.'

Teri was the nurse in charge of the dispensary, the only one of us who had access to the commandant.

'Yes, do that,' said Vera. 'Maybe she can help.'

I went to Teri. She was a Hungarian Jewess of

twenty-two, nice and kind. Moreover, she was pretty and intelligent and might possibly be able to influence Schara. She promised to try.

That evening I could not sleep. I could think only of Vera, her courage and strength. Now at last I understood her Mona Lisa smile. Her pregnancy had made it easier for her to endure imprisonment. I wondered if we would have a small child to take care of in the camp.

After several days of waiting, Teri had news: 'Schara has promised that Vera will be allowed to have her baby.' We could not believe it. 'It's true. You can give birth in the sick bay.'

Vera lifted her head. Her eyes widened and she gave a broad smile: 'Blessed be God.'

Now she became more communicative. In the evenings we sat on our beds and listened to her for hour upon hour. She told us of her beloved Zdenek, of her grief when they were parted, her suspicion of pregnancy which became certainty, of the baby which had grown inside her, her plans, her hopes, how she intended to care for it. As she sat and talked, she glowed, her blonde hair luminous in the weak lamplight. We tended and protected her, doing her work when we could and sharing our meagre rations with her. She needed them more than we did. But it was still not enough; we knew she needed more nourishment. And how would we clothe the baby when it was born?

I wrote to Paul and asked him for help. Next day I received a packet of powdered milk and a needle, and when I was clearing up after the bombing I found a reel containing several yards of cotton. Now I had only to find a piece of cloth, and I could make a little shirt. But where would I get that? We had no sheets, and our clothes were carefully inspected. We could not get fresh ones before we had handed back every item. We racked our brains. Each girl would approach her Frenchman, we would search in the ruins, perhaps Teri could provide some rags. But none of this led to anything.

I had almost given up hope when Paul received a parcel from the Red Cross. By a miracle it contained two handkerchieves, which he at once sent on to me. That evening we all helped to turn the two grey squares into a tiny shirt, the most wonderful little shirt I have ever seen. Now the baby could be born. Everything was ready.

And it came. A few mornings later we awoke to find Vera's bed empty. I ran to the sick bay, but she was not there. Teri was sitting there alone, staring emptily. Her face was ashen, her body hunched, her chin drooped on her breast.

'For God's sake! What has happened?'

She did not reply. She did not seem even to see me but just went on staring. When I shook her and repeated my question, the emptiness left her eyes and she looked at me in terror, as though she had just seen something even worse. Eventually she spoke.

'Dead!'

'Vera dead?'

'No, Vera is alive. The child is dead.'

I hugged and stroked her. 'Try to tell me, Teri.'

My touch seemed to release something in her and she began to cry. Her first words were unintelligible, but gradually I understood that when Vera's labour had begun, Teri was ordered to take her to the empty barracks. Schara came and witnessed the birth. Then he drowned the baby. Now she sat there incredulous that she had witnessed so inhuman an act. I knew I had to calm her, make her understand that it was Schara, not she, who had murdered the child.

I could not stay long with her, for the signal for roll-call had already sounded. The girls were lined up, and I did not want them to be punished for my absence, so I left her and went into the yard. The first person I saw was Vera. She stood in her line, thin, shaky and pale, her eyes dead. Everyone was looking at her; none dared speak. Not until we went to work could she tell me anything.

'I didn't even see him,' she whispered.

Poor Vera. Poor Teri. Which was the more to be pitied?

Vera could not work. Even the work leader could see that. So she was told to lay a fire in the guard-room. She wept unceasingly, and we had no words of comfort to offer. She could not understand that she had been duped. She thought she had been promised that she could keep the child. Time and time again she took out the little shirt and cradled it. When at last she could find words, she said: 'I don't wish none of this had happened. Being pregnant was the best thing that has happened in my life.'

The days passed, as if on a conveyor belt. It was good when nothing happened. But the SS men liked to shake us up. We were not allowed to enjoy peace for long. As soon as we became accustomed to a workplace, we had to move and begin again from the beginning – make new contacts among the prisoners of war, for their little packets meant all the difference between life and death. Another way to shake us up was by repeated bed checks. If a blanket was not correctly tucked in, we were punished, as of course we were if anything was found beneath the mattress. We tried to keep any little scrap we found; everything was of value to us who owned nothing. Many kept their morning's ration so as to have a little to eke out the midday and evening soup, only to regret their husbandry when they found it had disappeared.

Some weeks, or it may have been months, after Vera's tragedy, we were met on our return to camp by Schara in a rage. Our beds had been badly made, and bread and other things had been found in almost every one. We would be sternly punished. We would learn once and for all that he was not to be trifled with. The offenders were called out, among them Vera. Schara knew how to prolong a punishment, and after repeating that the penalty would be severe, he stalked off, leaving them standing to attention. A good while later he returned and announced: punishment work on Sunday. The yard was to be flattened, the uneven areas filled with earth, and the earth levelled with a roller. This would be a lesson to us that rules existed to be obeyed.

The next Sunday, after roll-call, the offenders were assembled in the yard and, after another sermon, were allotted their tasks. Some had to dig, others to spread the earth, and the hardest task, that of pulling the heavy roller, was given to Vera. Schara gave the signal to begin and posted himself to enjoy the spectacle. Vera went to the roller and began to pull. It was clear what force was needed to move it. She bowed almost to the ground, making a little bob backwards for every step she took. We wondered how long she could go on. But on she went, dragging the heavy roller forward and back, forward and back, with an expressionless face. Occasionally she stopped, took several deep breaths and dried the sweat from her forehead. Schara smiled contentedly.

At noon they were allowed half an hour's rest, to come inside and eat. Vera was completely exhausted, and we did not think she could go on. She herself hardly believed it. But she was driven out again; Schara knew no pity. Everyone had to go on. The rest of us could not help. We could only watch from our windows and try to will them strength. As twilight fell, I saw a team of ghosts toiling there. When the signal to stop work was at last blown, Vera collapsed in front of her roller. I ran out to help her. She had fainted. I got water and bathed her temples. When she came to, she said: 'I would rather die than endure another Sunday like this.' It was the first time I had heard her speak like that. Vera, who always thought of the future, who was always optimistic, who always looked forward to a life of freedom, however unattainable that might seem.

Her prayer was heard. By the following Sunday she was dead. She was one of those who died in the accident on Wednesday.

It happened so quickly that I had difficulty in discovering the details.

It was a period of much bombing, and Livi and I, with five or six others, were clearing ruins some way from the camp. We were taken there in a special tram, and Livi and I always sat in the front car with our closest friends. It was an unwritten law that sisters and friends kept together, sat next to each other, scarcely dared to let go of each other's hands. Anything might happen. We dared not challenge fate by letting each other out of sight.

It happened after work. The whistle was blown and everyone ran to the tram to claim their seats. Suddenly Livi shouted: 'Wait a moment. I must get something I hid under that brick.'

'Be quick. They'll grab our seats.'

'I won't be long.'

When she at last arrived, the tram was ready to go, and a furious SS guard shoved us into the last car amid oaths and blows. There was nowhere for us to sit. I said: 'You should have been quicker. Now we'll have to stand the whole way.' Livi did not answer but stared dreamily.

The tram started, and the exhausted girls talked softly, happy that the working day was done and that they would soon be back in camp to stretch out on the hard beds.

'Do you think we'll get jam today?' asked one.

'Could be. It's a long time since we had it.'

I didn't join in. Of course it would be good to have a

little jam as extra, but what did it matter? We'd still be hungry. It seemed to me that the Germans themselves had not much to eat. Our foreman today had cooked himself a soup from potato peelings. But at least he had some bread with it. Coarse, country bread with a rich, shining crust. I watched him hungrily, but he waved me away. Was he ashamed at not sharing with me or because he himself had so little? He must have known we had even less. But he was not unkind: he turned a blind eye when I went into the hut to warm myself. Although spring was on the way, there was a sharp wind, and it sometimes got very cold.

It had been blowing all day, and when I looked out of the window I saw that the wind had risen. The tram rolled slowly, and I searched for signs of spring in the trees that lined the road. I could see no buds. The trees were still bald, and nothing hid the open wounds the bombs had made in the surrounding buildings. Not many houses were undamaged. But now I was so used to this that the sight hardly moved me. A piano on its back with legs aloft made me think of my own piano. Where is it today? Is someone playing it?

Suddenly my thoughts were interrupted by an ear-splitting roar. A bomb, I thought. Now we were going to die. I grasped Livi's hand. She stiffened as the tram shuddered and stopped. We fell onto the girl opposite us and looked at each other in fear.

'What happened?'

In the silence I saw that the two cars in front of us had disappeared in a cloud of dust. A second later a great noise erupted, shrill screams blending with groans and weeping. I ran from the car to be greeted by a dreadful sight. Injured girls with blood streaming from them were lying on the ground or crawling among heaps of stone and fragments of tram. It was a moment before I realized what had happened. A bombed building had been blown onto the passing tram, smashing the two leading cars. Not the third; all of us who had been sitting there were unharmed.

I ran to a girl half-buried in masonry and helped her up. She had only scratches but was badly shocked. People began to pull out the wounded. We dug with our hands. Those who could get out by themselves staggered to the roadside, where they huddled like wounded birds. It was an age before anyone came with water and rags. Now at last we could wash and bandage the wounded. They groaned, begged for water and called desperately for their sisters or friends.

'Cipi, Cipi, where are you?' cried someone feebly, who had just been dug out bloodstained from a pile of rubble.

'Here I am!' shouted Cipi, happy that her sister was alive.

'My chest hurts so.'

'Lie still. You may have broken a rib. The ambulance will be here soon.'

It arrived. But the wounded were not allowed into it, only the dead. Schara, who had been informed of the accident, drove up and began to shout orders. The wounded were to be laid on the seats of the undamaged tram-car and driven back to the camp. They were not to go to the hospital but would be attended to in the dispensary, where they would get better or die.

It took a long time before everyone was accounted for. The wounded groaned and screamed. Most of us wept aloud. A woman was dug out who showed no sign of life. 'Mother, mother!' cried her thirteen-year-old daughter, whom we had all envied for having her mother with her. Now we could only pity her. To lose one's mother now was almost worse than to have done so earlier, when it had happened to all of us. She would not believe that her mother was dead. She hugged and kissed her, crying, 'Mother, mother, you mustn't die! You mustn't leave me!

Look at me, mother!' Livi went over to her and tried to calm her. It was only then that I saw that the girl herself was injured, one arm hanging lifeless, probably broken.

Another lifeless body was dug out. It was Vera. I could not believe my eyes. Vera, whom I had been talking to half an hour earlier. She could not be dead. I could not see any wounds on her, so I tried to give her artificial respiration, but to no avail. She was dead. Her prayer had been answered.

New Year's Eve 1944

We had just returned from work. Our evening meal was finished, our 'coffee' drunk, and we were chewing a few crumbs of bread. It was very cold outside, and the meagre sticks we had to burn gave little heat. I squatted on my bunk trying to warm myself as I listened to the others.

Someone said: 'It's New Year's Eve.'

'What difference does that make?' came from one of the beds.

'People are putting on their best clothes and getting ready for dinner,' said a third.

'Do you remember what fun we used to have?' said Magda.

'Only a year ago,' said Teri. 'But it seems like another life.'

The girls began to shed their apathy and join in. Almost everyone remembered something. Everyone wanted to tell of past New Year's Eves and happy memories.

'Do you remember the food we used to have?'

'Peter always brought lots of beer.'

'I used to be in love with Peter. I wonder where he is now. Do you think he's alive?'

'Sure to be. He's young and strong.'

'Do you remember that frilled pink silk blouse I looked so pretty in last New Year's Eve?' said Olga, pretty Olga, who now sat hunched and thin with a hedgehog stubble covering her skull.

'Lucky she can't see herself,' I thought. Last year she had been the queen of the ball.

'Is it only a year ago?' asked Bözsi, Olga's sister. 'It feels like a lifetime.'

" 'Eternity in an hour'',' said Magda, always ready with a quotation. 'Blake didn't have this in mind, though.'

They chattered; I listened. I too was overwhelmed with memories, but I found it too painful to clothe them in words. I began to understand Dante: *'Nessun maggior dolor ...'* There is no greater pain than to remember happy times in sadness.

The whistle blew and the lamps were extinguished. We did not want to sleep and lit a tallow candle which someone had managed to procure. We squatted on our beds and reminisced. Our memories were interwoven with poems and stories. Everyone had something to contribute. Rózsi began to sing. She had a soft, pretty voice, and several of us joined in the song. Everyone began to cry when she sang of the poor little girl who, dressed in rags, sold matches in the cold to passers-by.

'Belz, my little town, where are you?' came sadly in Yiddish from another bed. Another voice began 'Mein Yiddisher Mama'.

When we had wept our fill and ran out of songs, someone asked: 'How do you think 1945 will be?'

'The same as 1944.'

'Do you think we'll be here next New Year's Eve?'

'We'll never get out of here.'

'Perhaps we won't be alive.'

'We may die of hunger or be sent back to Auschwitz.'

'How can you talk such nonsense?' I snapped, adding with sudden conviction: 'Of course we'll get out of here.'

'When?' asked Sussie.

I replied instinctively: '15 April.'

The girls jumped from their beds and clustered round me. Suddenly I was regarded as an oracle.

'Is it true?'

'How do you know?'

'Do you promise?'

'Will the war be over then?'

One followed another. Everyone looked at me in wonder and admiration.

'Will the war be over then?' asked someone again.

'The war won't be over, but we shall be free,' I replied, again without thinking.

They looked at me in doubt, willing themselves to believe. Suddenly everyone was silent and thoughtful.

'Let's have a bet,' said Sussie.

'All right,' I said.

'What do I get if you lose?'

'My bread ration,' I replied without blinking. 'What do I get if I win?'

'How can I tell what will be worth as much then as a bread ration today?' said Sussie, seemingly impressed by my confident reply. 'But I promise it'll be something equally valuable.'

We sealed the bet with a handshake, put out the tallow candle and went to bed. Tomorrow would be an ordinary working day.

It snowed. The winter enclosed us in its iron grip. The cold grew worse every day. My clothes provided little warmth, and my shoes were in tatters. A rumour spread that a few pairs of boots had arrived and would be given to a lucky few. Who would get them? Only those with influential friends.

Those with special duties, in the kitchen or the dispensary or on the work site, were always first when any extras were handed out. The doctor, the *kapo* and the *blockova* were privileged, and I was nothing, someone with no rights and no hope of a windfall. But I could not but dream of a pair of shoes when I looked at my feet. There were great holes in the soles, and the uppers, or what had once been uppers, were held in place by bits of wire. Sometimes I had been lucky enough to find old newspapers in the ruins which helped to protect my feet from the cold. But not recently, and today I had only a flake of leather between my feet and the snow-covered ground. The wire that kept everything in place cut me with every step I took. I hardly knew my feet any longer: they were simply two lumps of ice on which I limped. Like a mirage I saw before me a pair of whole boots. I even began to imagine that my feet were warm. But how could I join the elite? Dare I go to the camp commandant? Anyway, he can't kill me for asking, I thought, and decided to take the risk. I would go to him, show him my useless shoes and ask for new ones.

At that moment I saw Schara in the yard. I braced myself, swallowed several times and went up to him.

'My shoes are finished. Could I have a pair of new boots?'

The blow on my left cheek threw me off balance. I staggered but remained upright and looked him in the eyes. That impertinence was too much for him. He raised his hand and hit me again, this time on the other cheek. I staggered again but still managed to stay upright, still somehow hopeful. But by now he had lost interest in me, and with a last contemptuous glance he turned and went.

That evening I prayed to God for a miracle.

Next morning the ground was deep in snow. When I arrived at the work site, the foreman looked at my feet and said: 'I've been looking at your feet for days. Your shoes are useless. Can't you get a pair of decent ones?'

'Some boots have come, but there weren't enough for me.'

He looked round cautiously. 'I've found a usable right shoe,' he said, and showed me a man's large brown shoe, which bore signs of having been dug out of some ruin.

'May I have it?'

'Would you like it?'

I would. Imagine: one foot not freezing. I put on the big brown shoe and had a sudden vision of myself as Charlie Chaplin. I lacked only the stick and the moustache. My right foot was in a kind of brown boat, my left in black tatters. My right foot began to perk up and seemed not to want to know its left neighbour, which squeaked resentfully. I dared not stand still and warm my left foot. If anyone discovered the foreman talking to me, he would get into trouble. I walked back to work bewitched by my feet. The brown shoe, the black tatters. I looked at them as I took one step after the other, beginning to doubt if they were mine. I felt split: it must be two people whose steps I was watching, a man who had been dug out of the cellar of a bombed house, and a beggar on the way to a charity institution to scrounge a pair of shoes.

It was a long time before I managed to change that left shoe. It did not happen until the spring, when a consignment of wooden clogs arrived.

That was a strange feeling too, to put on clogs, shoes made entirely of wood. They were difficult to walk in. I soon developed blisters on both my heels and the upper part of my feet. But they were better than my old shoe. I no longer felt the snow and slush under my soles.

We made an odd sight marching in our new clogs, stiff and awkward. We still had our civilian clothes with the yellow crosses, but now that spring was on the way we had to hand in our winter things. I missed my blue coat, for the air was still chilly. I had a brownish-yellow check dress with long sleeves, Livi a black skirt and a beige jumper. This last she had begged from another girl; it had originally belonged to our cousin, Livi's best friend, Ditsi, and had been knitted by her mother. When she saw it on the other girl, she naturally wanted it and was ready to make any sacrifice to swap it for her own red one. To own a garment that had belonged to a relation felt almost like having that person there.

Often we wondered if Ditsi was still alive somewhere in the camp, or whether she was dead. Much later we learned that she had stayed at Auschwitz and was shot during the evacuation. That was the hardest thing to accept, that someone had gone through hell to no purpose and had died just before being liberated.

The days passed. Another and another. I did not know what date it was. Sundays I recognized, for then we did not have to work. But this did not mean rest; on the contrary, these days were more tiring. We had to stand and freeze at endless roll-calls, whereas work at least enabled us to keep a little warm. In the evenings I used to mutter a small prayer which I had adapted from the Hungarian poet János Arany:

> I thank Thee, God,
> For night again.
> One day less
> Of earthly pain.

We looked forward to sleep. I tried to imagine that sleep was the reality and the days a dream, a nightmare from which I would awake as soon as I fell asleep at night. Then I could see my loved ones again, talk to my boyfriend, eat the best food my mother could cook and walk in our garden among the flowers and fruit trees. In the mornings I told Livi what I had seen during the night, and counted the hours before we would meet our parents again in Sighet. She listened without comment but wanted to know every detail – how mother looked, what she was wearing, what food we ate, how the garden looked. All this I told her as we marched to work in the sharp wind and biting rain.

Usually we walked casually instead of marching in time as our guards wished. So they ordered us to sing marching songs, and any of us who failed to keep time felt the whips. They wanted passers-by to see a happy workforce, not a bunch of stragglers. It was wise to please them, so we sang and marched as best we could. Arriving at the workplace, we continued singing as we began to clean up after the night's bombing, a song that seemed exactly appropriate: 'The world lasts only for a day.' 'Who knows what waits us, what tomorrow brings?' one girl would sing, a line from a banal Hungarian hit song. But this depressed us, so Rózsi changed to a more cheerful German tune: '*Es geht alles vorüber, es geht alles vorbei*' – 'Everything passes', and we all joined in.

Soon we began to believe the words we were singing, and our voices rang out cheerfully. The guards became uneasy and tried to silence us, but when we stopped, the song was taken up by other groups working nearby, and when they were silenced, we began again. Eventually the SS men lost their temper and threatened to shoot us. This had its effect. We had not expected such a strong reaction; we only wanted to vex them and did not dare to make them angry.

Our main task was to cheer each other up. We kept together, supported and lent strength to each other. Most of us had known each other since childhood, and I dared not think what would have happened had we been parted. I think we would have lost the will to live. When anyone weakened, there was always someone to turn her mind to other thoughts. We felt responsible for each other, kept each other's hopes alive.

5   Life Goes On

One cold but sunny winter day Kati and I were sent to chop wood in the forest close to our working site. It was hard work, but I liked it. I liked getting into the forest and away from the noise. Wilhelm, the only guard who occasionally showed human feeling, accompanied us.

It was early morning, and we watched the sun rise as we marched towards the forest. The pines were weighted with snow. Chopped trunks lay around. Our job was to cut off the branches and saw the trunks into logs that the next group could take back to heat the guard-room. As we worked, we saw a little old woman in a black shawl standing behind a tree, in front of a little hut. She looked closely at us, went back into her hut, then came out again and, as soon as the guard had turned his back, beckoned invitingly to us. She repeated these gestures several times. I wondered what she wanted.

'Kati, do you see that old woman waving to us?'

'She seems to want us to go to her.'

'We'd better not. It might be some trap.'

'What trap? She's only an old woman.'

'No one else has ever dared approach us. Why should she?'

'We can try to go closer and see what she wants.'

We watched her but did not dare go to her.

'Look! Now she's beckoning again.'

The old woman went back inside. After a moment she returned with something in her hands. Was it a sandwich? It looked like one.

The day passed, and we cast furtive glances at her as she continued to beckon and go in and out of the hut.

Towards evening, we decided that Kati should distract the guard's attention while I approached the old woman. I began to gather the logs, walking in ever wider circles. I remembered that we were sometimes allowed to keep branches and twigs for our own stoves in the camp, so I asked Wilhelm if I might do this. He nodded, and after a moment I gave Kati the signal. She began to give Wilhelm a long account of her schooldays, which she knew interested him. He had been a schoolteacher before the war. I summoned my courage and slipped over to the old woman. When I had come within speaking distance, she whispered: 'Don't be afraid. I too am Jewish.'

I could hardly believe it and again feared a trap. She pointed to her house. Now I could see that the table was laid with a white cloth, on which two candles shone in simple wooden holders, while on a plate rested something which looked like a covered loaf. Challa? Everything suggested preparations for the Friday evening meal, Shabbat. Perhaps she is a Jewess after all. But how can she be here, at liberty? How can she have escaped the SS? Perhaps she has Aryan papers and lit the candles only for us? Or was hope blinding me? I didn't know and couldn't ask. I dared not dally, took the proffered sandwich and ran back.

Back in the camp no one would believe me. The sandwich was not sufficient proof.

The whole night it snowed, and next day my group and I were sent by tram to the station to clear the streets. The morning sun shone on the ruins around, but the station itself was, amazingly, intact. Its clock showed ten past eight. We worked silently. Between spadefuls I blew a little warmth into my frozen fingers. The deep snow muffled the sounds around us. We scarcely heard the few vehicles we could see. Red-cheeked people in warm clothes hurried by, seemingly unmindful of us, though they could not help throwing a glance in our direction. What did they think when they saw us, skeletal women in thin clothes stooping to shovel snow? Or did they not see us? One doesn't see what one does not want to see. A few people stopped and watched, but no one came near or asked questions. Later they would say they knew nothing. And, later still, that it was all a lie.

We shovelled snow all day, with a break for soup at noon which warmed us for a while. Otherwise we kept up our body warmth by working harder, but it was difficult to stop our hands and feet from freezing. We stamped our feet, swung our arms and stuck our fingers in our mouths. Even so, many got frostbite. But eventually that day too ended.

The next day was Livi's fifteenth birthday. Birthdays were not allowed to pass unnoticed, even in the camp. I discussed it with the others and decided we would celebrate in the evening after work. She must of course know nothing beforehand.

In the morning I hugged her and wished her many happy returns. I said I was sorry I had no present for her but promised to make up for this later, when we were free. She did not say much, but I could see she was disappointed. That was part of the plan. She will be all the happier in the evening, I thought.

The day passed as the previous one had, sweeping snow in front of Hamburg station. Livi was quieter than usual, no doubt thinking of earlier birthdays, of our parents who always woke us with songs and chocolate in bed, of presents we had had, and parties. There would be no party this birthday. But when we got back from work, Sari, who lived in another barracks, called her over on some pretext, so that we could arrange our surprise.

I laid a small fir branch in the middle of her bed, and around it we placed our meagre presents. A shoelace, a stub of soap, a broken tin with beauty cream in the bottom. We had scrounged a few treasures from the ruins. Sussie gave her jam ration, and Magda a poem she had written for the occasion. I was able to provide a bread ration which I had saved up over several weeks. We decorated the bed with more fir branches and cones and awaited her arrival. When she came, we sang 'Happy Birthday'.

Livi's amazement was something to behold. 'Is all this for me?' she asked. She was too overwhelmed even to thank us. Going to the bed, she picked up each object and repeated again and again, 'Mine. For me. I've got presents. You remembered my birthday. Oh, bread!'

She lifted the bread and looked at me.

'Yours?'

When I nodded, she said: 'No, I can't take it. You mustn't give away your bread.'

'I've been saving it for a long time. Don't worry about me. It's my birthday present to you, and you must eat it all yourself. You mustn't offer it to anyone. Not even me.'

She looked at the other presents. 'Jam! Oh, thank you – whom shall I thank for this?' She saw the proud look in Sussie's eyes and hugged her. 'Bread and jam! What a feast!' She unscrewed the twisted tin and sniffed the contents. 'Beauty cream!' She embraced the donor, Olga, and at once began to rub it on. 'How could you know my face was so dry? So dry it hurts. And soap! And a shoelace! What treasures! How can I thank you all? You're all so kind. And I've nothing to give any of you.'

The girls from the kitchen brought coffee, and we sat

around Livi waiting for her to eat the bread. Someone lent her a penknife she had found, and she cut off a slice so thin as to be almost transparent. Slowly and ceremoniously she spread it with a very thin layer of jam. Eight pairs of eyes followed her smallest movement.

'Spread it a little thicker. You don't have to save this. You must eat everything tonight,' said Sussie.

Livi spread a little more and bit into it blissfully. As it disappeared into her mouth, I too began to chew. I was not conscious of it until I saw her eyes fasten on me, and then I noticed that all the others were chewing too. Livi stopped eating and made to offer the rest of the bread to us. I stopped her. This was her birthday and her bread, and no one else might touch it. Not even I. But she could not eat while the eight pairs of hungry eyes followed every bite. In the end each of us had to accept a morsel. That was how she wanted to celebrate her birthday.

More and more often now we heard from Paul and the other prisoners of war that Germany was on the point of capitulation. This news affected us like vitamin-injections. After each such injection the reality was harder to bear, but the warm spring sunshine made us feel easier and gave us a glimmer of hope. It was late March. Hamburg was being bombed almost incessantly.

Paul's letters told me that the Russians were nearing Berlin. In coded language he wrote that he did not intend to await the end in Hamburg, and asked if I would like to try to escape with him. He suggested that I slip out of the camp during an air raid, when the guards would be in the shelter. He was afraid for my safety, fearful that the Germans would kill us before the liberating army reached the camp. He thought he could use his knowledge of the city and lie low until it was freed.

I gave it much thought but, after talking it over with Livi, decided that the risks were too great. The SS guards always set their dogs loose before going down into the shelter, and threatened to shoot anyone who left the barracks. Of course there was a risk in staying – Paul's fears for us might well be justified – but the energy that escape would require was more than I possessed. I could only follow the line of least resistance. What must be, must be. I wrote to Paul wishing him luck and promising to contact him if we should both survive.

Two days later there was great activity in the camp, and the rumour began to spread that it was to be evacuated. The Soviets were approaching – or was it the British? – and our tracks had to be covered. We wondered only how they would do away with us. We had no doubt that now we were to die. Our guards seemed to think the same. We were summoned to roll-call and stood waiting there for several hours. Eventually the commandant arrived and ordered us to crowd together into one of the barracks, all 200 of us in a room which had hitherto housed twenty girls. We sat on the beds, wondering what they would do to us. The crush reminded us uncomfortably of the situation in the synagogue prior to our deportation. Would they deport us again? Or just kill us? No one spoke. We waited.

After a while, an SS woman, fat Marie, came and ordered us to undress. We obeyed. When someone asked why, she explained that where we were going we would need no clothes. We embraced each other. One question burned in my mind. How will they murder us? By shooting? When two girls came with the soup, I thought I knew the answer. Poison. We mustn't touch the soup, I thought. But what then? If they mean us to die, we must die some way. I saw no escape.

Just then the camp commandant entered and looked at us in surprise. He began to shout at us. Why were we all sitting there naked? When he saw fat Marie, he bawled her out and ordered that our clothes be returned to us. She obeyed sheepishly. She seemed disappointed that she was not about to witness a mass execution. We dressed again and went on waiting. It felt a little better not to be naked.

I remembered an old Jewish story. A poverty-stricken father, living in one room with his seven children, goes to the rabbi for comfort and is counselled to bring his goat in to join them. When the crush and stench become intolerable, he can throw out the goat, and then everyone will appreciate their little home. I did not exactly appreciate our situation, but felt calmer.

After some hours we were taken out and transported to the station in the evening darkness. I thought again of Paul. I wondered if he had managed to escape, and if I had been right to stay. The future would show.

It was 4 April 1945. We were in a freight train again. The old fear enveloped us. Sealed goods waggons with shutters nailed over the windows. Will they gas us after all? We must wait and see. The train stood in the sidings all night. We dared not sleep. A weak light had begun to filter through the cracks in the shutters when the train at last started. The whistle shrieked and the engine coughed its way into the dawn. As the day passed, our fear was exacerbated by hunger and thirst. The excrement bucket in the corner was soon full and running over. The stench made me feel sick. We had seen all this before. I turned to look for my mother but saw only the pale faces of my comrades in grey. I comforted myself with the hope that there is a life after death and that I would soon see her again.

It was twenty-four hours since we had last eaten. Our water had long since given out. No one spoke. The train grunted on, stopped, restarted, stopped. The day was far advanced when the waggon was at last opened. We were ordered to empty the bucket and get drinking-water from a nearby pump. Then the waggons were resealed. We filled our hungry bellies with water, despite a warning that we would be wiser to ration it. None of us knew when we would next see water.

The sealed train stood still as night fell. We sat crowded and fearful, listening for the least sound outside. We still had no idea where we were going, but it was easier to endure when the train was moving. I tried to will it to start, but it did not move. Suddenly we heard a rattle. A waggon door was thrown open and I heard a volley of shots. So this was the answer, this was what they had planned. We are to be let out, one waggonload after the other, and shot in the night. Livi and I clasped each other and waited, not daring to move. Perhaps they will forget us if we are really quiet. We sat there waiting, but nothing happened. The night was silent. No other noises were heard. But we dared not sleep.

Towards dawn the train started and crawled on into the unknown. Another day passed, and another night. On the third morning the train stopped. The doors were opened. I was blinded by strong sunlight. I heard birdsong and, as my eyes became used to the light, I saw deep green before me. Broad fields, grass, trees. Where have we come to? Are we still alive?

Harsh shouts of command assured us that we were still with the SS. When we climbed down from the train, we found ourselves facing a camp surrounded by barbed wire and bearing above the gate the now familiar words '*Arbeit macht frei*'. Inside stood pale and listless ghosts.

'Where are we?' I whispered to one of them.

'No gas, no bread, much work,' came the terse reply.

So, I thought, perhaps we still have a chance. We had become used to going without food and were still able to work. If there was no gas chamber here, there was hope.

Later I learned we were in Bergen–Belsen.

6   Bergen–Belsen

7 April 1945
We were led into the barracks, which were not unlike those at Eidelstedt, and were allotted a bed each. We fell on them at once, exhausted and starving after the long journey.

For a long while nothing happened. We waited, hoping for food. The afternoon passed, but no one bothered about us. Eventually some girls came from the kitchen with a cauldron of soup. When my turn came, I tried to will the girl into dipping down to the bottom. Vegetables, perhaps even a little meat. She dipped the ladle, filled it and poured into my bowl a brownish, smelly liquid that seemed mostly water with a little vegetable. Cabbage? Onion? I could not tell. But after three days without food it felt good at least to perform the functions of eating: dip the spoon in the soup, then put it into my mouth, swallow and feel the hot liquid run through my body. I ate slowly, to make it last. We got no bread.

In the evening we were summoned to roll-call, and again in the morning. Otherwise nothing happened. In the morning we were given 'coffee', at noon a thin soup, and 'coffee' again at night. After a few days we got bread, but only once. We never saw bread again there. Nor were we given water. Many of the girls went outside and drank from the filthy puddles in the yard, although this was forbidden; for fear of typhus, or just to torture us?

One day on my way to the latrine I saw on the other side of the fence a woman in rags approach a puddle. The guards at Belsen were mostly Hungarian soldiers, and I heard one of them shout to the woman to halt. She paid no attention and bent down to drink. A shot rang out and she fell.

One morning an SS man entered the barracks and asked if anyone wanted to volunteer for work. This would be rewarded with an extra bowl of soup. I volunteered, without any idea of what the work might be. We were taken behind the barracks, where big heaps of bodies lay scattered, given spades and told to dig deep graves and bury the dead. I looked at the corpses and set to work without any feeling. They could as well have been logs of wood. I did not even reflect that I might have been among those lying there.

My skeletal companions and I dug vigorously. When the SS man whistled for lunch, I was completely exhausted. We were given a thick soup with vegetables; mine even included a meatbone. When we had finished, I noticed there was a little left in the cauldron. I thought I would take some to Livi. I queued again and when my bowl was filled put it aside, thinking how happy this surprise would make her.

As I sat and rested, the bowl seemed to talk to me, tempting me to change my mind. 'How good I smell, how thick I am,' it seemed to say. But I steeled myself. This was for Livi, however much my stomach cried for it. But the soup continued: 'She's only lying on her bed. She isn't doing anything. You're working. You need more food. Drink me up, quickly. There may be enough for a third helping, and you won't have a bowl to get it. You'd be stupid to miss an extra helping by not having an empty bowl.'

This last argument I could not resist. In hope of a third helping, I drank this second one. I did so slowly; now that my worst hunger was satisfied, I could relish each spoonful. I held it in my mouth and savoured it for as long as I could before swallowing it. When I had finished, I looked up and waited for the next distribution. But no. The soup was finished and the girls from the kitchen were gathering the bowls to take them back.

I sat there with a full stomach and a gnawing conscience. I had cheated my young sister. I had drunk her soup. I was the lowest of the low. Just like the others. I had thought only of myself. With what loathing had I despised those who cheated their sisters or stole from their mothers. Now I was no better. Could I ever make amends to her for this betrayal? I felt I had cheated not only her but our mother, who had entrusted her to my care.

But we had all changed. Most for the worse; some for the better. Some had shown themselves to be noble and selfless. I shall never forget Maria, a servant girl who discovered her old mistress in the camp. How selflessly she tended her, always prepared to go hungry until the frail old lady got something to eat. And my own aunt, whom I had never liked because she was so selfish and nasty to us children. She had no children of her own, and we always thought she did not like us. But now she changed completely. She looked after her niece Judith as though she was her own daughter. Whenever she managed to arrange a little extra of anything, she gave it to Judith. Judith herself told me this after the war.

But such were the exception. Most people thought only of themselves. They could hit their mothers and steal their sisters' bread. Now I felt like one of them.

15 April 1945
We are lying apathetically on our beds. Someone asks:

'How long have we been here?'

'Who knows? A week? A month? A year?'

'What date is it?'

Someone said: 'The fifteenth of April.'

'Pity,' I said. 'I've lost the bet. Sussie, you'll have to grant me credit. We shan't get any bread today.'

Sussie hardly had the energy to answer. We were no longer hungry, only incredibly weak. We lacked the strength to make any unnecessary movement, utter any needless word. I just lay there: I don't think I even had a thought in my head. I felt as though I was floating in a void. Was this what they call Nirvana?

As the day went on, there was a sudden noise outside. The girl nearest the window shouted hysterically: 'British tanks!'

Poor child, she has become delirious, I thought. I did not bother to look.

Some hours passed. Then fresh noises were heard from the yard. Someone in one of the upper bunks sat up, looked through the window and cried: 'Look! Look! The soldiers are running!'

'They have white armbands,' said another.

'Look, a British soldier!'

Something was undoubtedly happening. With difficulty I got to my feet and tottered to the window. I saw – or was I dreaming? Had I too begun to hallucinate? I was not sure, but I thought I saw uniformed soldiers who were not Germans. We had been liberated. And it was 15 April.

At that moment I felt only an indescribable weariness. I walked back to the bed and wanted only to sleep. But suddenly my mind began to work. I began to plan tomorrow. Tomorrow, tomorrow I shall look for Father. 'He is alive. He must be alive. I feel it.' I tried to persuade myself, and thought back to the time when we had sat on the train for Hamburg and a girl had come with a greeting from Szmuk.

There was silence in the barracks. The whispers of joy had ceased. Most of the girls were already asleep, exhausted.

'Tomorrow, tomorrow, we shall begin to live.'

Tomorrow I could go round the various camps. No guards, no barbed-wire fence could stop me from looking for my father. I would comb one camp after the other. As I drowsed off, I saw myself climbing through fences as though they were spiders' webs. Now we are free.

Freedom. I could not fully grasp what this might mean. But one thing I knew: I am alive, having been dead. I died the night of 17 May 1944, the night we came to Auschwitz. But now I am alive again. I have been granted a second ration of life. Henceforth I shall celebrate my birthday on 15 April. Who knows what kind of life awaits me? Whatever happens will happen to another me, who has nothing left of the girl who was born in Sighet one June day in 1924.

When the next day dawned, no one stayed in her bunk. Weak as we were, we went out into the yard to see what had happened. Each of us was driven by something stronger than herself. Most of us went in search of food and drink, I of my father. This was the thing that once more saved my life.

We were starved and desiccated. The British soldiers stared at us in repulsion and pity, as though unable to believe their eyes. How should they? These walking skeletons – 'Mussulmans' as we called ourselves, thinking of fakirs – were we living human beings? They had never seen anything like us. Prisoners of war they had liberated, but not living corpses. They wanted to help, and when anyone begged for food they gave it generously. They gave their rations – tins of ham, baked beans, thick soups: rich, heavy food, good for soldiers. They were full of kindness; how could they know that starving people must not eat such food? Doubtless they were happy to see gratitude and joy shine from our previously dead eyes as they gave all they had. But the stomachs of those who accepted their gifts reacted with deadly effect. All developed dysentery. Many died.

We did not know at the time what caused the first attacks of diarrhoea. A rumour spread that the Germans had poisoned our last bread ration, or put powdered glass in it. Not until much later did I realize that it must have been the rich food and the dirty water. Now that the guards were not there to prevent us, everyone drank from the puddles.

I could not think of food or drink, and so escaped the rich contents of the British ration tins. I got a few beetroots from a kind soldier and, fortified by them, began to wander around. The gates separating the various camps were demolished, so I was able to walk from one barracks to another. I met several men from Sighet, but none of them knew anything about my father. I also came across the sister of my former boyfriend Puiu, lying on a pile of rags, ridden with lice and dying. She gave me a weak smile of recognition, and a little spark came into her eyes when I promised to return the next day with food, soap and clothes. Next day she was dead.

I did not find my father. But I found Michael. He was sitting by a fire grilling five potatoes a soldier had given him, and as soon as he saw me he gave me three. He had gone to Auschwitz in the same transport as we and was able to tell me that my father had been sent to the left and that it had been my Uncle Alex who had sent the greeting from the bakery, the only one of my father's brothers and sisters to survive.

So father was dead too. I could not cry. I had no tears left. I had wept them all.

Wandering around the camps, I became infected. I

coughed and was feverish but refused to accept that I was sick. There was so much I had to do now that we were free. I had to organize food, clothes, necessities. I worked until I collapsed. There were no army doctors about, so Livi searched out one of ours, a liberated prisoner who had worked as a doctor before the war. He himself was more dead than alive, enfeebled with dysentery and very weak. Laboriously he dragged himself to my bed and examined me abstractedly. He diagnosed typhus, from which most of the prisoners were now suffering. I felt very ill and longed to hear that my fears were exaggerated.

I said: 'I think I am going to die. My heart is beating so hard, it seems to want to jump out of my throat.'

He looked at me with pity but showed no sign of wanting to contradict me. I read in his eyes: 'I am sorry for you, but when so many are dying, what does one more matter?'

I turned to the wall and waited for death. The fever increased, and I felt as though I was floating in a giant balloon which grew bigger and bigger. The balloon and I floated together, and I knew that when the balloon burst I would vanish too. I was drenched in a cold sweat. After that I do not remember much more, except that one morning I opened my eyes and found I was not dead.

A long convalescence followed. Livi tended me with wonderful patience. She forced me to get up and take a few tottering steps. I learned to walk again. My young sister had become adult in a night. She took charge, organized food, cooked nourishing soups and nursed me back to strength. I don't know how long this took, but she succeeded. Slowly, slowly, I regained my legs. Each day I became a little stronger, and at last I was well. Only then did I learn that we were no longer in the barracks but had been moved to what had been the soldiers' quarters outside the camp. Then they told me that the whole camp complex had been burned by the British.

The occupying powers took charge of us. They gave us good rations of bread daily and soup twice a day. But our hunger was not easy to satisfy. We needed more. To obtain more food, and other things beyond bare necessities, I decided to find work. I heard that the British were generous to anyone who helped with the administration of the camps. I knew a little English, so I went to the authorities and asked if they needed an interpreter. They did, so I was sent to the Welfare Office, where a group of woman officers was working under the leadership of Mrs Montgomery, sister-in-law of the general. I was accepted, to translate from Hungarian into English and vice versa. I was also to do odd jobs such as cleaning, running errands and making tea. I thought expectantly of what might fall from the rich man's table. That first day my hopes were answered, for I was allowed to take home everything that was left from the ladies' tea. When I unpacked milk, sandwiches, jam and a hunk of cake, my friends looked at me as though I was Father Christmas.

We seven, who had kept together since leaving Hamburg, had become a little family, and since I had found work I was regarded as the provider. We took on roles. Teri, who was good at cooking, became mother, and the rest sisters who lent a hand, each according to her ability.

The most precious commodity at this time was cigarettes. Smokers longed for something real after their home-rolled efforts with leaves and newspaper. Camel and Philip Morris appeared like mirages. Those of us who did not smoke sold what we could get dearly. The soldiers gave generously, and soon cigarettes became a hard and sure currency. They could buy anything. A slice of bread cost five cigarettes, a piece of meat ten. I did not smoke and saved every cigarette I could lay my hands on. In the evenings we sat around my bed, brought out our cardboard box and counted our assets. Mostly we used them to buy food, occasionally clothing. We went to the nearby village and took all the food and clothing we could find. It did not feel like stealing. We had been robbed of all we possessed and were simply taking a little back, that we might have something to put on our backs and fill our ever-hungry stomachs with.

One Friday morning, when I was about to leave for headquarters, I saw Livi getting ready to go to her work. The thin, leggy girl whom I still thought of as a child was seated in front of a mirror making herself up. She rouged her cheeks, applied lipstick, brushed her again-luxuriant hair and practised ogling looks.

'What are you doing?' I asked.

'Making myself pretty.'

'Why do you have to look like that?'

'What do you mean?'

'Made-up.'

'You know it's easier to get a Tommy interested if you look pretty. Otherwise they won't notice me. How else can I get cigarettes?'

I did not think she understood the implications, and tried to explain, but she would not listen.

'What does it matter if they kiss me?'

'But suppose they want more? What will you do?'

'Push them off, of course.'

'But if they persist?'

'Then I'll hit them.'

I could not sway her. She was determined to make her contribution and provide some of our necessities. And she succeeded. Her childish naîvety survived her make-up, so that the British soldiers understood why she had painted herself. She returned laden with cigarettes, a live hen and several shirts.

'How on earth did you manage?' asked Teri.

'I went to the main road and walked towards the village. You know most of the houses have been deserted since the Germans left. I saw some shirts drying on a line, and as no one was living there, I thought no one needed them. You and Rosie have no shirts, so here's one for each of you. Then I walked on and met a lorry with some soldiers. They stopped and asked where I was going. I told them, and they gave me a lift. They agreed that I had a right to the Germans' belongings, and said they had taken things from German officers and given them to ex-prisoners. They were nice. One especially, called Jim. He was very nice. He gave me chocolate and though I don't smoke he gave me a whole packet of cigarettes to take home. He promised to come here on Sunday with some tins and stuff. Then I walked round the village to see what I could find. I saw a hen scratching in the ditch, and no one seemed to be looking after it, so I took it and here it is.'

With a triumphal expression she held up the terrified hen. She, the youngest of us, was providing our first chicken dinner. Now we could prepare a real Shabbat feast, we could buy flour with our cigarettes, bake Challa, cook chicken soup and light the two tallow candles I had got from a British soldier earlier in the week.

That evening we sat round the table, which was laid with a white cloth which Sussie had somehow acquired, and saw the Shabbat candles dance in the dusk. We blessed and ate the Challa, Teri served out the soup and meat and, as we ate, memories began to awaken. First one, then another told of earlier Shabbat feasts, and we sang songs we remembered from our childhood. We wept a good deal, longing for our parents, and hugged each other, grateful that we had each other.

The weather grew warmer, the sun shone and the birds sang to us in our new-found freedom. I was a young girl again. One interest eclipsed all others: boys. This was true of all of us. We weighed no more than sixty-five or seventy pounds and still had not begun to menstruate again, but our hair had grown, and that was the main thing. We felt ourselves women again, put on lipstick and tried to charm the British soldiers. Small romances began to blossom, which sometimes led to small tragedies. We had been ripped from our families and now, consciously or unconsciously, were driven to seek new bonds.

Several of our friends were in hospital. Their enfeebled bodies could not stand much and were plagued with various illnesses. Most had typhus, or colds which developed into pneumonia, or tuberculosis. I did not think much about them. I was selfish. The only one I occasionally visited was Magda, who had diphtheria. She had looked forward so much to freedom. But, hungry as she was, she had eaten greedily of the rich tinned food and next day suffered a severe attack of dysentery which turned to diphtheria. She was taken to the military hospital, where they diagnosed an inherent heart condition. This was why she was now dying. When I visited her, her only wish was to send a greeting to Vera, whom she had found just before she fell ill. Vera was her favourite cousin and the only survivor of her family. I promised, although I knew that Vera had died of typhus the day before. As with so many families, no one was left, no one who could return to Sighet, tell of the family's fate and start a new family.

But we who survived would do that.

I don't think we were conscious of this aim. Even Bözsi acted out of character. She was the eldest of us and, according to her sister Olga, had never previously shown any interest in boys. She was not beautiful. She had a freckled face, a pointed nose and a lantern jaw. Her hair was red and sparse; her skin shone through it and made her look as though she was still bald. She held herself badly, and when she walked, her thin body looked like a sickle wielded by an invisible hand. We had no chairs and had to sit on our beds, but no one was allowed to approach her bed. When any girl who visited us unwittingly did this, she raised her tired voice in a falsetto and scolded the offender. But if a man sat down, she walked up and down in front of the bed and flirted with him. She said nothing, just looked happily at him and caressed him with her narrow, watery eyes.

Olga was much sought-after. Her splendid hair had grown again, and her sunken cheeks had begun to fill out. Her skin shone again like ivory, her eyes glowed clear, and her merry laugh put us all in a good humour. She was naturally flattered that most of our male visitors came because of her. But she rejected one romance after another. One never knew who was in favour. She would agree to meet one admirer but go out with another. We enjoyed her triumphs, though several of us were jealous.

Life flowed easily in the former barracks. On the surface it seemed almost normal, a woman's world of gossip and intrigue, centred on food and men. We thought neither of the past nor of the future. Only today mattered: filling our bellies, and a little romance. But we knew that in time we would return to Sighet and reality.

Sussie was troubled. She did not know what to give me for the bet I had won. But she was ill, and I calmed her by telling her that I was happy to wait.

7   A New Beginning

3 July 1945

We were sitting in the train from Lübeck to Travemünde. It was getting towards evening, and the few of us who had not gone to bed were chatting in the carriage. The train ran on through the German landscape, and we scarcely cast a glance at the moorland passing by the window. What had been was past. Now the future beckoned. A new life awaited us. The impossible had happened: we had survived.

The conductor entered the carriage and asked in German: 'How are you girls?'

'Fine,' I said. 'But it would be nice if we could lie down. We are very tired.'

'I don't know if there are any sleepers free. I'll have a look.'

'Can I come with you?' I asked. 'My cousin's in one of them. I'd like to say hullo to her.'

We walked down the train. The sick lay in second-class sleeping-compartments. The looking-glass in the corner, which not so long ago had reflected the confident looks of officers returning on leave, now mirrored these emaciated faces and lifeless eyes. Eventually we found Sussie, lying on a bunk with another sick girl. Sussie was pale and weak, a shadow of the shadow I was used to. Her skull was bald. Typhus had robbed her of her hair. When she saw me, she tried to smile, but her voice was scarcely audible.

'Good of you to come. Will it be long before we get to Sweden?'

'We get to Travemünde in the morning, then we take a ship to Malmö. It may take a few days.'

'Do you think I'll make it?'

'Of course you will. The worst is over now. They'll look after us in Sweden. You'll soon be well.'

'How lovely your hair is. Look at me. I've hardly any left.'

'You'll get it all back when you're well. It'll grow again.'

'You really think so?'

I tried to sound confident, though I was not. But talking tired her and she fell silent. I sat on the edge of her bunk, took her bony hand and stroked the parchment-like skin. I did not know what to say. I hoped she would get well. I thought of Magda, who had been in the room next to hers in the hospital at Bergen-Belsen. She had died on 2 July, the day before we left. As though reading my thoughts, Sussie asked: 'How is Magda?'

'Getting on,' I said. I did not dare to tell her the truth. She would learn in time. Just now she needed all her strength.

The train whistled and stopped at a station. I got up and looked out at the deserted platform. A solitary workman stood there with a red flag, turning his curious glance from me to the red cross on the train. Did he know who we were? Probably not.

The whistle blew and the train started. I sat again on the edge of the bunk, listened to the wheels and tried to interpret what they were saying. 'She'll – get – better – she'll – get – better – she'll be well, she'll be well,' they sang, as they picked up speed. I looked at Sussie to tell her what I had heard, but the monotonous thumping had already sent her to sleep.

I returned to my compartment. The others were sitting as

I had left them, chattering, laughing, dreaming. They had so much to tell, these new friends: their childhood, their loves, their dreams. Everything except what they had just left behind them.

We were six girls in the compartment. Two from Sighet, and four from Satu-Mare. We had felt drawn to each other when we learned that we should all be on this train. We got on well, were about the same age and seemed to have the same interests.

Adela talked of the books she had read and the courses she intended to follow when she got back to Romania.

Isa told of her experiences in her Communist group, of the anti-Fascist work she had done before the deportation and which she intended to continue. She was the eldest of us and was still fired by these ideas. She described the millennium that awaited us, and kept repeating, 'Remember, girls, what has happened must not happen again. Only Communism can prevent it.'

Her sister Rella was silent. She revered her big sister and never dared speak in her presence. Anyway, she was too young to have anything to tell which could impress the big girls. But she had dreams, which she wanted to realize. She dreamed of going to school, of learning something and becoming something, not just a shadow of her big sister.

Kati talked mostly of her elder brother Gyuri and her hopes of seeing him again. Her dreams centred on helping him and others in need of help. She was the one who always thought of others, the altruist among us self-centred egoists. We were preoccupied with our own problems.

When I came in, they were discussing what had happened in Lübeck, after we arrived there from Bergen-Belsen. I saw again the big tent where the Swedish Red Cross had made us shower and change our clothes.

We and our clothes had to be disinfected before they would send us on to Sweden.

'Do you remember that handsome Swede who came into the tent when we were in the shower?' said Livi.

'Odd that men washed us. I felt ashamed standing there naked,' said Rella.

'I talked with that Swedish girl Marianne who was with them,' I said. 'She says it's normal in Sweden for girls and boys to bathe naked together. In their bath-houses they have female attendants who scrub the men, and quite often men wash women. It's very strange.'

'What kind of a country are we coming to?'

'They must be nice. Their queen has invited us for a holiday. A girl on the train said she'd heard that the queen herself is going to meet us at the frontier, to give us all fine new clothes and a gold watch each. Even an evening dress.'

'But what will the food be like? They're so thin, these Swedes. Do you think they'll give us enough to eat?'

'They know we've been starved. They'll give us enough. We'll be honoured guests. After all, they've invited us.'

'I'm going to take a double helping of everything, and put some aside in case they don't feed us often enough.'

'Do you think they can cook food as good as we got at home?'

'You won't taste mother's meatballs again,' I said. 'But I'll make some as good for you as soon as I get the chance. I remember how she used to prepare them.'

'How can you remember?' asked Livi. 'You were only a child.'

'Have you forgotten who did the cooking when mother was away? When you were sunbathing by the river?'

She remembered and was cheered.

'Where is Sweden?' asked Rella.

'I think it's the left half of that dog-shaped thing on the map,' said someone.

What else did we know of Sweden? That the king played tennis and that the people were so honest that you could leave your door key on a bench and go back and find it several hours later. That was all. And later we found that what we thought we knew was wrong. No queen to meet us, no watch, no holiday. Not the left half of the dog. And the honesty? That stopped before we arrived. The only thing that was true was that the king played tennis.

But what beautiful people! I admired the conductor on the white bus that fetched us from Bergen-Belsen. If all Swedes look like him, things will be dangerous. I shall fall in love with all of them. He was tall and broad-shouldered, with deep blue eyes. And nice. Unfortunately we couldn't talk with him, as he knew only Swedish. When they talked among themselves, it sounded like singing. Shall we ever learn this language? But we shan't need to. We didn't plan to stay long. Six months, then back to Romania.

The guard came back to take us to some empty compartments where we could stretch out. Livi and I lay down together and began to fall asleep. I put my arm round her and saw from her eyes that she was dreaming again of her Karel. Karel, the Polish boy whom she had fallen in love with in our last days of Bergen-Belsen and who had gone to Sweden by an earlier transport. I saw that in her mind she was reunited with him. It was because of him that we two were on this train. I had not been able to endure her sadness, and managed to fiddle permission for us to come to Sweden, although both of us were well.

When the rumour first spread that the Swedes had invited the sick to convalesce in their country, we did not think much about it. Livi and I would soon return to Romania and continue our education. I would at last fulfil my dream of studying medicine, and she would matriculate. Then, as our cousin Sussie was very ill, we were told that she would be taken to Sweden. A few days later Livi came to me in tears with the news that Karel would be going too. She did not want to be parted from him. He was her first love, and it was very serious. Couldn't we do something? Might we go too?

Without thinking much of the possible implications, I went to the Swedish Red Cross people and asked if we might be allowed to accompany our sick cousin. The Swedes were generous. They did not want to separate relatives. So we were put on the list.

Only then did it occur to us that this would mean being parted from our friends, Teri, Olga, Bözsi, Rózsi, all of whom would stay behind. It was hard to leave them, but we consoled ourselves with the thought that we would all soon meet again in Sighet.

Then the excitement began. Questions. Discussions. Rumours. Our imaginations ran riot. It was so easy to believe in rumours that promised something positive. We stopped washing our few items of clothing. There was no point taking anything with us, as we should get all we needed as soon as we arrived in Sweden. Some girls had managed to get new clothing and were now relatively well dressed. But now that we were on the way to Sweden we might as well throw away everything we had.

When we arrived at Lübeck we had only the clothes we stood up in. Most of us were wearing what we had had on when we were liberated, rough garments with a yellow cross on the back, torn and dirty. All this was burned by the Red Cross people while they disinfected us. Then we were given new underclothes, a summer dress and a pair of shoes. No evening dress, and no nightwear. We accepted the absence of an evening dress. We would not need one on the journey; that would doubtless be given to us when we reached the frontier. But nightwear? Why did we get no pyjamas? What were we to sleep in? To our great surprise, the Red Cross man replied that he always slept naked. We accepted his argument, noting it as yet another of this strange country's eccentricities.

In Lübeck I met a middle-aged British sergeant. He was pleased to find that I spoke English, and invited me for a walk in the park. Delighted that anyone showed any interest in me, I accepted gratefully. He asked about what had happened to me, and told me of his own tragedy. His wife had died, and their motherless child awaited him in Yorkshire. He felt sorry for me, and sorry for himself, and asked if I would marry him. I almost said yes on the spot, without reflecting that I did not know him, that he was much older than I, that I knew nothing about his background. My hunger for a family, to feel that I belonged, to share my life, was such that I would have done anything to still it. But first I wanted to discuss it with Livi. I was unwilling to part from her.

It was fortunate. She looked at me with her big child's eyes and asked: 'Do you love him?'

'Of course not.'

'Why marry him, then?'

'I want a home.'

'We're going back to Sighet. That's our home.'

That decided me. Next day we continued our journey to Sweden.

In the morning Livi and I returned to the compartment in which we had sat the night before. The other girls were there, more or less rested. I sat by the window and looked at the landscape. Ruins everywhere, signs that the war had raged here too. It occurred to me that others had also suffered, but I could not feel pity for the people who had lived in these shattered houses. I saw halved houses standing: a bedroom with a bed; an upturned dressing-table and a broken mirror; a kitchen with a saucepan on a stove; the remains of a living-room, where someone had once read a newspaper and listened to the wireless. Had he been an SS man? I liked to think so. I called to the others, and we began to fantasize about the people who had lived in these houses.

The more we talked, the more we felt how much we had in common and how similarly we felt. I dreaded the possibility that we might be separated on arrival, and the others said they felt the same. So we solemnly vowed that we would always stay together to help and sustain each other. We would be each other's parents, sisters, friends. We seven would live together; Sussie would, of course, join us. When I told her this, she smiled and nodded agreement. She had no strength to share our dreams.

Time sped, and we were still planning our future when the train reached Travemünde. We were put onto the ferry that would take us to Sweden – a white dove on its way to Paradise. I sat on the deck and would have liked to stay there looking at the sea. But this was not allowed. We had to go below and rest. We were given breakfast and a beautiful bed each, with paper sheets. This proved an odd experience: when I lay down in the rustling bed, I felt like an expensive chocolate. Is this what life is to be like? From now on, shall I always be treated like a luxury and wrapped in cellophane?

8 Sweden

9 July 1945

We have landed in Sweden.

Was it Ystad or Malmö? It must have been Malmö. I remember only that we went ashore to be met by uniformed women – WAACs as I later learned – who offered us hot chocolate. Hot chocolate for me always stands for Sweden. They manifested good will, care and attention to our physical needs. But we also longed for affection and tenderness. These needs would doubtless soon be answered too.

The sick were taken to sanatoria, while we who were well were quartered in a school to undergo six weeks' quarantine. We were each given a bed and a dressing-table and installed in a big, bright classroom.

For the first few days we did nothing but eat and sleep. We ate and ate, and when we were not eating we talked of food. Most of us stole extra portions from the dining-room and hid them in case we should be hungry again. Soon the odour of decay began to spread from the various beds, and the authorities started a campaign against hoarding. We were forbidden to take food out of the dining-room. But this ban was not respected. Then they gave us pocket money, and we had to promise that we would buy what extra food we needed from the kiosk between meals. We spent most of this on white bread. It was a long time before we dared to accept that there was food enough to spare, and stopped hiding pieces beneath our pillows. Some of us never did.

We were isolated while they waited to see if any of us was infected. Curious citizens of Malmö crowded round the school fence and stared at us as though we were from Mars. Their faces expressed pity blended with mistrust. We were grateful for any words addressed to us, any expression of sympathy. We were not allowed to stand by the fence and talk in case our bacteria might cross it, but day after day the curious citizens returned. Ultimately we ignored the ban. Here were people who cared. Friendships sprang up, and addresses were handed to us, with a promise that we would meet as soon as we were released from quarantine.

After some weeks we regained our strength sufficiently to protest against being confined within the fence. We felt imprisoned. The authorities tried to calm us with the assurance that the quarantine was for our own good and that the fence was there to keep snoopers at a distance. We found it hard to accept this. We had had enough of isolation and wanted our freedom. My companions discovered that it was easy to crawl under the fence and began to slip out for a walk in the town or a visit to a friend.

Two Swedish sisters, Ingrid and Barbro, got into the habit of coming to the fence to talk to Livi and me, in our only common language, German. They were the same age as us, and we became friends. We wanted to know everything about their family. One day Ingrid asked if I would like to visit them, as soon as we were allowed. I said I would, and at once. Without giving her time to wonder, I slipped under the fence.

I looked round. I was on the street. I walked a few hesitant paces and looked back. I was alone. I looked back again, and again. It was hard to believe that I was alone. It took time before I dared to be sure that no SS man was behind me with a rifle and that no one would shout at me to halt. At that moment I at last realized that I was free, and what this meant. No more soldiers to guard me, no more degradation. No one would ever again control my life. No more persecution of me as a Jew. It will never happen again. The world has learned a lesson. They have understood.

I began to walk more assuredly, almost skipping forward as I accompanied Ingrid to the suburbs of Malmö between smiling villas with gardens of flowers. I passed a lilac bush whose boughs overhung the fence, and pulled off a branch. Ingrid looked at me in disapproval and said warningly in German: 'One doesn't do such things in Sweden.'

We came to a yellow house, where we were met by Ingrid's parents, a middle-aged couple not unlike my own parents. Ingrid introduced me, and her mother invited me into the living-room and offered me hot chocolate and sandwiches. We began to talk, but her warmth changed to a chilly unease when she learned that I had left our quarters without permission. One doesn't do such things in Sweden, I was reminded again. If I was to stay in this country, it was made clear, I would do well to respect its laws. But her curiosity overcame her mistrust, and since I was here, would I not tell them what I had been through?

Where shall I begin? Auschwitz? Would they understand?

'I am a Jew.'

'But why did they send you to the concentration camp? You must have done something?'

What does one reply to that? That we have done nothing? That that was why we were imprisoned? Had we done something, we would have been shot. And we hoped to avoid that by doing what we were told. We had been brought up, generation after generation, to be good and obedient. Father knows best; if a child is disobedient, she is punished; if she follows the rules, no harm will come to her; if the neighbours are nasty, there is always Father at hand. In new situations, one always falls back on the old order of things. Few can imagine a situation which they have not experienced. And those few are never believed.

With mixed emotions I drank my chocolate and asked Ingrid to accompany me back to the school.

August 1945

It is a fine summer day in Stockholm. The afternoon sun, mirrored in the waters of Lake Mälaren, blinds the passers-by and brings perspiration to the foreheads of the panting cyclists. No one seems to be in a hurry as they cross the bridge. The only sound is the gentle pinging of the gliding trams. No cars are to be seen.

I stand leaning over the bridge. A thin teenager with a stubble of hair and a hungry look, I am wearing a green silk dress which I have made from an old curtain, in early forties style. It is cut well above my knees. I feel very smart in it and hope no one notices my feet. I am a little ashamed of my black laced shoes and short white socks. Patent leather shoes and silk stockings would have been smarter.

I look at the view, dazzled by its beauty. A sudden unease makes me turn round. No, no armed SS guard stands behind me. The pavement is empty. Behind the bridge is only a shining mirror where the sunbeams chase each other.

Where am I? How did I come here? Just now I don't know. I am filled only by the recurrent, joyous thought: I am alone, I am free, free to go where I please, free to do what I please, free to enjoy the day as much and as long as

I please. I look around thirstily, I want to drink the greenness, the sun, to swallow everything at once. I want to gulp down everything quickly, quickly, as I have been gulping bread these last weeks, quickly, before anyone can take it from me.

My eyes meet the old town on the other side of the bridge. An improbable fairy city rises from the water. Enchanted houses line the shore, winking at me with their window eyes. Those behind lean forward and beckon, leading me to the fairy palace of my childhood. The palace itself glows ruby red, its gilded cupola glittering in competition with the water. A seagull circles the tower, and the three crowns set their seal beneath the invisible writing on the blue sky. I dwell on the picture, unwilling to be parted from this fairy tale.

The sound of the tram swinging round a curve makes me turn slowly round. Inquisitive eyes meet me from the tram's windows. Men and women, contented, well fed, seemingly happy. On their way somewhere, to someone waiting for them: father, mother, friends. A small cloud shadows the sun for a second. No one is waiting for Livi and me. But the thought passes before it can take root. Just now there is only this wonder, this strange feeling which is so new that I scarcely recognize it. Joy? Happiness? Is this how they feel?

Laughing girls come towards me. Their skirts reach far below their knees. A tandem drives past, a father in check shirt and red tasselled cap, a mother in shorts, a child on the handlebars, another in the basket. How funny they look.

Beneath the bridge sit two small boys. They too wear red caps. They have rods in their hands. One threads worms onto his hook, the other casts his line in a broad arc. A bucket stands beside them, and I wonder if they have caught anything. I want to go down, to ask if I can be with them and tell them that I too stood under a bridge long, long ago. Perhaps a hundred years ago, perhaps in another life. Before my world vanished. Or, rather, before I vanished from the world.

But now I am back. A splinter of womanhood in a short skirt. And I don't really understand why everyone is looking at me. I don't understand that it is I who am different, I who look strange. Someone from another planet. In my hurry to live I imagine that I can go on exactly where I left off, with my skirt far above my knees. I have not realized that one cannot go on as though nothing has happened, even regarding the length of one's skirt. It will take time before I understand this.

Today I am full of the wonder that meets me. Sweden. Stockholm. So much water, so many bridges. Tall buildings. Trams that run through grass. Dogs that never bark. Children who never cry. Neighbours who never quarrel. Hardly any police anywhere. Quiet. Clean. Orderly.

In the country which I come from, everything was different. Throngs of people, sounds and smells, disorder, mud and dirt on the streets. No tall buildings. No trams. Hardly any bicycles. I had never seen a tandem. A summer day there could be as glorious, yet how different. When I think back, I smell the dust and see the sky which was so much closer, bluer. Is it that a child's heaven is always bluer?

But the time of childhood is past. I am grown up, and life is waiting. I do not yet know if I shall survive, but I know that I want to. What has happened can never be forgotten, but I must not think about it, not now. I would rather think of our beautiful stay at Hjälmared, where we regained contact with the nature which we had missed for so long. We lived in a school, walked in the forest, swam in the lake, lay in the sun and ate.

To eat: that was the most important thing. There were still many of us who found it difficult to lose the habit of hiding food. It was this hoarding that caused the row with our supervisor, Kalle. Plus the difficulty of ridding ourselves of 'organizing'. We still had only the few items of clothing we had been given on our arrival at Lübeck, and the sight of sheets and check mattress-covers made us envisage an increased wardrobe. We cut most of them into pieces and sewed for dear life. Soon we all had new summer shirts, shorts, skirts and dresses. Kalle was understanding but could not stand aside and see school property destroyed in this way. He called a meeting and rebuked us. We understood his viewpoint, but 'organizing' had entered into our blood, and it was hard for us to rid ourselves of it. Much later, when I was living in Stockholm under so-called normal conditions, I still found myself wanting to 'organize'. Quite unceremoniously I picked up an apparently abandoned bucket of coal from a cellar, and only several moments later realized what I had done.

The weeks at Hjälmared rolled past, and in August we were moved to a camp on an island named Lovön near Stockholm. The camp comprised a number of barracks separated from the rest of the island by a barbed-wire fence. Sussie was well again, and we seven, friends since Bergen–Belsen, moved together into barracks no. 7.

There we awoke to reality. Summer was approaching its end, and with it the end of our holiday. It was made clear to us that we were no longer guests. We were refugees. This word was new to us, and it did not feel nice. From having been a temporary guest, with a supposed home elsewhere, I became insecure, small and helpless, wholly dependent on the good will of others. We sat in the barracks and discussed for days on end whether to return to Sighet or stay in Sweden. Apart from Sussie, none of us had any family left in Sighet, and the thought of returning to an empty house, to a town from which we had been expelled, seemed as difficult as to stay where we were. In the end we decided to stay – at least for the time being.

Life in the camp made me restless. I wanted to get out, to freedom. I wanted to be rid of my badge of refugee. I would use all my energy to get away from Lovön as quickly as possible and began to explore the possibilities. Again my knowledge of English proved useful. The only way to gain permission to be resident in Stockholm was to find household work, and I found a job with a family who wanted English taught to their children. So I turned my back on camp life for ever.

15 June 1949

We met in front of the registry office. I had on a blue woollen dress with a long skirt, in the latest 'New Look' mode, a short rounded jacket and a white straw hat shaped like a millwheel. I felt very smart in my new dress, which had cost me a whole month's pay, and was happy in my borrowed hat. Michael was elegant in his new grey pin-stripe suit and grey-blue tie, my present to him. He hugged me, looked at me with his big grey-green eyes and smiled. The sun broke through the clouds; all my grief and suffering disappeared. His dark, bushy eyebrows invited me to stroke them. I felt that I wanted to follow him to the world's end, that I had at last found a home, found my husband, my father, my brother, all in one person – my companion for ever. He had the rings but no flowers.

'Do you want some flowers?'

'Er – yes.'

'Come on then. We'll buy a bunch.'

We crossed Bergsgatan to a little florist's and chose a bouquet of lilies of the valley. My favourite flowers. I took a deep breath and inhaled their perfume. Small moments of happiness, to seize and cherish and keep carefully, to bring forth when life again strikes with its hammer.

Our hardest years were behind us. Housework, factory work, office work. We had managed to teach ourselves Swedish and now both had relatively well-paid secretarial jobs. Since Michael had also succeeded in finding a flat, we thought we could marry. We were from the same town, had the same background, the same experiences, the same longing for a family. What did it matter that he was so much older? We loved each other, understood each other and could give each other strength. We would have a family and bring up children with values other than those in which we had been brought up. The children would be assured and bold, they would be loved for what they were, and we would never try to change them. But one thing we would not renounce. Our children must know that they were Jews, and bear that knowledge with pride.

August 1985

The cars stand still on the West Bridge, their radiators boiling in the heat. My eyes run along the line of traffic and come to rest on the bridge. I see the image of a skinny girl leaning over the parapet. I close my eyes and remember. How everything has changed since then! The city and the girl. The sun shines as brightly, the sky is as blue. The trams are gone, no families ride on tandems; no pedestrians, hardly any bicycles. And no red-tasselled caps. Correctly dressed businessmen in their cars on the way home from work, with no thought that this might be in any way remarkable. Most of these young company directors who sit nervously smoking or drumming their fingers never knew the carless West Bridge of forty years ago.

Forty years! A lifetime! An extra ration, another spoonful of life which I was granted on 15 April 1945.

I was a leaf that floated on the sea of life, thrown hither and thither, brushing against other wind-driven leaves. I met Michael, and the roots of our two thin saplings entwined and slowly, slowly found life. The storms abated, but the tree survived and grew into a broad, strong oak that brought forth branches and flowered in this foreign land. Until the storm struck again and took half the trunk.

I did not think I would survive. I died every night. Yet each morning I awoke. It took a long time, but the wound healed and the memory gave me strength to go on.

The extra spoonful which life offered me also gave me a duty. I pondered for a long time what might be the meaning of this extra ration, this new life. It took me forty years to realize that I am a witness and that it is my task to tell what I experienced, although I am not a writer. We who survived are so few. We must tell of this inhuman thing that was done in the twentieth century. It must not be forgotten. And it must never happen again.

I still remember, but hardly know how it felt. I remember that it hurt, but I can no longer recall the actual feeling. I remember the infected toenail. I remember the shame when I stood naked. I remember the moment of goodbye. I still remember most of it, but the memories fade. If they fade in me, how will it be with those who never experienced it? And later generations: will they be able to understand?

Epilogue

Another summer has arrived. After the endless Swedish winter I am again astonished that the ice has melted, the cold has ceased and the birches are leaping into bud. More than forty years have passed. I am sitting in the country surrounded by my three sons and their families. My seven grandchildren romp and play, and I think how happy Michael would have been to see them.

My three sons have become clever scientists, loving fathers and very loving sons. Of course we have had our differences. I was perhaps stricter than I would have wished. I had to be both father and mother, stern and gentle, and this was sometimes a problem. It was harder for the boys than for most others of their age, for to lose one's father is not something one can ignore. I was determined to give them the upbringing, the start in life, that Michael wanted for them. His words rang always in my ears: 'They must be brought up to be good human beings. They must keep their Jewish identity. We have been persecuted because we are Jews. Our children and grandchildren shall be proud that they are Jews.'

When Michael died, on Yom Kippur, the Day of Atonement, 1962, for a long while I obeyed the law of least resistance. The little business of supplying hospital equipment, which he had started when it became apparent that he would not be able to follow his former profession of lawyer in Sweden, was still running at a loss. We had big debts and I had to give up my psychology studies to help him. After his death I tried to carry on the business. To my amazement, increased orders began to come in, and by the end of the first year I was able to show a small profit. This increased annually, enabling me and my sons to lead a normal middle-class life. Once the boys had gone to university, I was able to continue my own interrupted education. I sold the business, went to university and took a degree in psychology. Then I was able to fulfil a plan which Michael had cherished. When we first came to Sweden, we missed the café life which is so much a part of Central Europe. There was no place where people could meet, drink coffee, read a newspaper, talk for an hour. Now, forty years later, the Jewish community in Stockholm has a place for those who survived but still have to fight the shadows of the past. A day centre has been founded, in which I work as organizer and psychologist and where former prisoners of the concentration camps can meet to drink coffee or take part in group therapy.

My sister Livi also lives in Stockholm. She married a German-Jewish refugee and had three children. She helped me through the hard years. We have summer cottages close to each other and share the joy that, despite everything, we are alive, our line continues. On occasions of celebration, twenty-eight of us sit round the family table. Stockholm is now our home; this is where we live, where we belong, where our children were born. Sighet, a little town far away, belongs to another life.

In June 1968, when my sons were in their teens, I took them on a trip to Sighet. Ironically, the Russians had liberated the area as early as January 1944, only eight months after we were deported, and had returned it to Romania. After a period of chaos a more or less liberal regime was established, though sadly this did not last for long. I wanted to show my sons the town of my birth, the places where I had played, the cemetery in which their ancestors lie. It was like turning the leaves of an old book, seeing a play one knows well. Everything was familiar, the setting was the same, only the actors were different. Strangers sat behind the counters in the shops, strangers drank coffee in Anna's garden. The cabs were still horse-drawn, but it was not Uncle Salman who drove them. As I approached Uncle Hillman's house, I thought I saw him walk out through the door. I ran up behind him, but a stranger turned and stared at me. The only person I knew in the town was Teri.

I did not dare to release any feelings. I had to leaf quickly through the book, watch the play without letting my emotions become engaged. But the visit had one good result. Until then, I had often dreamed that I was being kept in Sighet while Michael and the children were in Sweden. Now these nightmares ceased.

Five years later I went again to Sighet, this time with Livi. We needed to make a pilgrimage. We visited our old house, which I had not dared to do on the previous occasion. It was occupied by a Hungarian couple of about my age. They allowed us to look around but were distant and taciturn. Doubtless they feared we might reclaim the house, as we were legally entitled to had we decided to resettle in Sighet. It was in shabby condition. We went up to our attic, and my old feelings returned across forty years. I felt a child again. I looked through the window at the garden. The jasmine and lilac bushes were gone. I wanted to tell my parents, but they were not there.

What happened to the other girls from Sighet?

Dora returned, married Tsali, the man she had loved, had three children by him and emigrated to the United States. She is now a successful doctor in New York, with five grandchildren.

Sussie also returned to Sighet, married and had a son. Her husband was killed in an accident. She now lives in Hawaii, where she has remarried.

Teri married in Sighet and still lives there. To her great grief, she has had no children.

Olga married one of her admirers in Bergen-Belsen, an American soldier. Today she is divorced and is a successful businesswoman in Chicago.

Her sister Bözsi went to Israel, married and had six children. She died in 1980.

Anna lives in Montreal with her husband.

I do not know what happened to the others.